how2become

A POLICE OFFICER
The Insider's Guide

HODDER
EDUCATION
AN HACHETTE UK COMPANY

Orders: Please contact Bookpoint Ltd, 130 Milton Park, Abingdon, Oxon
OX14 4SB. Telephone: (44) 01235 827720, Fax: (44) 01235 400454. Lines
are open from 9.00 to 5.00, Monday to Saturday, with a 24-hour message
answering service. You can also order through our website
www.hoddereducation.co.uk

British Library Cataloguing in Publication Data
A catalogue record for this title is available from the British Library.

ISBN: 978 1444 107869

First published   2009
Impression number   10 9 8 7 6 5 4 3 2 1
Year   2015 2014 2013 2012 2011 2010 2009

Typeset by Servis Filmsetting Ltd, Stockport, Cheshire
Printed in Great Britain for Hodder Education, An Hachette UK Company,
338 Euston Road, London NW1 3BH by Cox & Wyman Ltd, Reading,
Berkshire.

Hachette UK's policy is to use papers that are natural, renewable and
recyclable products and made from wood grown in sustainable forests.
The logging and manufacturing processes are expected to conform to the
environmental regulations of the country of origin.

CONTENTS

INTRODUCTION

Welcome to *how2become a Police Officer: The Insider's Guide*. This guide has been designed to help you prepare for, and pass the tough police officer selection process.

The selection process to join the police is highly competitive. Approximately 65,000 people apply to join the police every year. But what is even more staggering is that only approximately 7,000 of those applicants will be successful. You could view this as a worrying statistic, or alternatively you could take the view that you are determined to be one of the 7,000 who are successful. Armed with this insider's guide, you have certainly taken the first step to passing the police officer selection process.

The guide itself has been divided into useful sections to make it easier for you to prepare for each stage. Read each section carefully and take notes as you progress. Don't ever give up on your dreams; if you really want to become a police officer then you *can* do it. The way to approach the police officer selection process is to embark on a programme of 'in-depth' preparation, and this guide will show you exactly how to do that.

The police officer selection process is not easy to pass. Unless, that is, you put in plenty of preparation. Your preparation must be focused in the right areas, and be comprehensive enough to give you every chance of success. This guide will teach you how to be a successful candidate.

The way to pass the police officer selection process is to develop your own skills and experiences around the core competencies that are required to become a police officer. Many candidates who apply to join the police will be unaware that the core competencies even exist. As you progress through this guide you will find that these important elements of the police officer's role will form the foundations of your preparation. So, the first step in your preparation, and before we go any further, is to get hold of a copy of the police officer core competencies. They will usually form part of your application pack but if they don't, you can obtain a copy of them by visiting the website of the force you are applying to join.

If you need any further help with any elements of the police officer selection process, including role play, written test and interview, then we offer a wide range of products to assist you. These are all available through our online shop www.how2become.co.uk. We also run a one-day intensive Become a Police Officer course. Details are available at the website www.PoliceCourse.co.uk.

Once again, thank you for your custom and we wish you every success in your pursuit of a career as a police officer.

Work hard, stay focused and be what you want . . .

Best wishes

The how2become team

The how2become Team

PREFACE

by author Richard McMunn

In 1993 I joined the Fire Service after serving four years in the Fleet Air Arm branch of the Royal Navy. After spending 16 successful years in the Fire Service, I decided to set up my own business and teach people like you how to prepare for a specific job. I have passed many different job applications and interviews during my life and I have also sat on the opposite side of the interview desk. Therefore, I have plenty of experience and knowledge that I will be sharing with you throughout this guide.

Throughout my career and working life I have always found that if I apply myself, and focus on the job in hand, then I will be successful. It is a formula that I have stuck with for many years, and it has always served me well. This kind of approach is one that I want to teach you over the forthcoming pages of this guide, and I hope that you will use my skills and knowledge to help you achieve the same levels of success that I have enjoyed.

Personally, I do not believe in luck when applying for jobs. I believe those candidates who successfully pass the police officer selection process do so because they thoroughly

deserve it. They have prepared well and they have worked hard in order to improve their skills and knowledge.

I have always been a great believer in preparation. Preparation was my key to success, and it is also yours. Without the right level of preparation you will be setting out on the route to failure. The Police Service is very hard to join, but if you follow the steps that I have compiled within this guide then you will increase your chances of success dramatically. Remember, you are learning how to be a successful candidate, not a successful police officer!

The Police Force, like many other public services, has changed a great deal over the years and even more so in how it assesses potential candidates for police officer positions. The men and women of the UK Police Force carry out an amazing job. They are there to protect the community in which they serve and they do that job with great pride, passion and very high levels of professionalism and commitment. They are to be congratulated for the service they provide.

Before you apply to join the Police Force you need to be fully confident that you too are capable of providing that same level of service. If you think you can do it, and you can rise to the challenge, then you just might be the type of person the police are looking for.

As you progress through this guide you will notice that the core competencies required to become a police officer are a common theme. You must learn these competencies, and also be able to demonstrate them throughout the selection process, if you are to have any chance of successfully passing the selection process.

CHAPTER I

HOW TO PASS THE POLICE OFFICER SELECTION PROCESS

Before we move on to the different sections of this guide, and in particular each element of the selection process, it is important to explain to you how I intend to teach you to pass the police officer selection process.

To make it easier to explain, we will break down your preparation into the following key areas:

Learn about the role of a police officer

Before you begin to even complete the application form, it is essential that you learn about the role of a police officer. This is for a number of reasons. The first reason is that you want to be 100 per cent certain that this job is for you. I know a few people who have joined the police only to leave a few months later because 'it wasn't what they expected'.

The second reason is that it will help you to pass the selection process. If you understand what the role of a police officer *really* involves, and not what you may *think* it involves, then you will find the selection process far easier. This is particularly true in the case of the role-play/interactive exercises and also the final interview (if appropriate).

There are a number of ways that you can learn about the role of a police officer. To begin with you will find some useful information contained within this guide. Secondly, you will find plenty of information on the website of the force you are applying to join, and also through the website www.policecouldyou.co.uk.

When reading this guide, and visiting these websites, take notes on the information you learn about the police officer role. This will enable you to gain an in-depth understanding of the role and in turn this will make the selection process far easier to pass.

Learn and understand the core competencies

The police officer core competencies are the blueprint for the role of a police officer. Just as the foundations for a house must be a firm base, the core competencies are the basic skills that a police officer must be able to master if he/she is to be capable of performing the role competently.

Throughout this guide I will make continued reference to the core competencies and I cannot stress enough how important they are. During the selection process you will be assessed against the core competencies at every stage, therefore you must learn them, understand them, and most importantly be able to demonstrate them at every stage of selection, if you are to have any chance of succeeding.

It is important that you obtain a copy of the police officer core competencies prior to completing the application form. You will also use the core competencies during your preparation for the assessment centre and also the final interview, if applicable.

Apply the core competencies to every stage of selection

During the preface I stated that you are learning how to be a successful candidate, not a successful police officer. Once you pass the selection process, the Police Force will train you to become a competent member of their team. During selection they are looking to see whether or not you have the potential to become a police officer and they will use the core competencies as a basis for assessment. At every stage of the process you must demonstrate the core competencies and I will show you how to achieve this.

Improve your fitness levels

Surprisingly, most candidates who fail the selection process do so during the fitness tests. They concentrate so much on passing the assessment centre that they neglect the other important area of fitness. Within this guide you have received a free bonus section entitled 'How to get police officer fit'. You will find some useful exercises contained within this guide, so make sure you set aside sufficient time to improve your fitness levels. Do not settle for scraping through the fitness tests but instead look to excel. You will find that as your fitness levels increase, so will your confidence and concentration levels. This in turn will help you to pass the selection process.

I strongly believe that if you follow the simple steps above, and you apply the remainder of the information that is contained within this guide, then your chances of passing the selection process will increase tremendously.

CHAPTER 2
THE ROLE OF A POLICE OFFICER

The first step on the road to passing the police officer selection process is to learn as much as possible about the role. On the following pages you will find brief details about the role and your training. The information provided is for example purposes only and you must check with the force you are applying to join that it is relevant to you. In addition to reading and absorbing this information, I recommend you visit the website of the Police Force you are applying to join, and also the website www.policecouldyou.co.uk.

The great thing about the life of a police officer is that you have the ability to make a difference. On many occasions you will change people's lives by your own actions. It is a demanding but highly satisfying career, which will provide you with the opportunity to make a difference to your community. You will be challenged daily but will have the tools and skills to be confident in your own ability to do the right thing.

Working in the Police Force is a challenging job, with many rewards. It provides the opportunity to perform a wide range

of roles and to take personal responsibility for helping others. The service strives to treat everyone fairly and you should also be prepared to do the same. Dignity and respect are key elements of a police officer's working life. There is no greater feeling than bringing offenders to justice, especially if it has involved hard work, gathering information, intelligence, identifying the offender and making the arrest.

Unfortunately, for every offender there will be at least one victim and the arrest means nothing if justice in a court does not follow. In order to bring offenders to justice successfully you will need to carry out your job competently. This will mean following correct policies and procedures as well as creating accurate and concise paperwork. When all these aspects come together you know then that you've joined a very special team.

Police officers are responsible for maintaining law and order, and providing a service to the public that ensures their safety, well-being and the security of their property and possessions. Above all, they are there to serve the community and this principle is the basis of all policing policy within the UK. The police are not there to control society, but rather work with society in order to reduce crime and make the community a safe place to live.

It is important that you remember that you are there to serve the public and you don't think that life as a police officer is all about catching and convicting criminals. You must be prepared to have the community's interests at heart, which is why you will be assessed against this important element during the selection process. Duties of a police officer can include patrolling on foot or in cars, investigating crime scenes or attending incidents and interacting with your community. Of course, there will be times when you need to work on the administrative side of the role and also be prepared to spend time in court giving evidence. Once again you will be assessed against this area during selection.

Being a police officer is certainly a demanding and responsible job. The rewards are that you can help prevent crime and protect the public, but policing can also frequently be emotionally taxing

and challenging. You need to ensure that you are prepared for this side of the job. You might be called on to tell a mother that her daughter has been injured or killed in a road accident, or endure verbal abuse while investigating an incident. During my career in the Fire Service I attended many incidents where a member of the public had sadly lost their life. I did not envy the police officers who had the task of breaking the terrible news to the families and relatives of the victim. In order to carry out this part of the role you will need great skill, courage and sensitivity. Once again, you will be assessed against this area during the selection process. Finally, it can also be an extremely physically gruelling and demanding job. For example, you might spend five hours on the beat in extremely cold conditions. Therefore your fitness levels must be good enough to withstand the demands of the job.

The most common reason that the UK Police Force turn people down is due to their lack of physical fitness. While the tests are not very difficult, you must prepare well for them. Your free information guide on 'How to get police officer fit' will go some way to helping you prepare for these tests.

In total, there are 43 police forces and more than 126,000 police officers in England and Wales – about one for every 400 people. In Scotland there are eight police forces. The person in charge of each force is a Chief Constable, except in London, where the Metropolitan Police and the City of London Police are each headed by a Commissioner.

As well as responding to more than 6 million 999 emergency calls each year, the police must contend with a vast array of crimes, from simple assaults to complex fraud.

Police probationary training

Once you have successfully passed the police officer selection process you will undertake a long period of intensive training that is designed to develop you into a competent police officer. Your initial recruitment training will last about 30 weeks

and it is a combination of classroom based tuition and on-the-job training which is carried out under the supervision of an experienced officer. Once you have spent sufficient time under supervised patrol you'll then be permitted to go out alone providing you have passed the necessary assessments and examinations.

I will now provide a more detailed breakdown of a police officer's probationary training. Please note that the following information is provided as an example only and should not be relied upon to be accurate.

The initial police officer training course

The two-year probationer training programme is made up of a number of key stages, which may include some of the following:

STAGE 1 – An introduction to policing

During this stage of your initial training you learn about the police officer's role. You will also learn how to provide a high level of service to the public whom you'll be serving. During this initial stage you may also learn additional key skills such as driving.

STAGE 2 – Training centre (approximately 12–15 weeks)

During stage 2 of your training you will gain an in-depth knowledge of the law and how it relates to your role as a police officer. You will also learn how to deal with a wide range of operational incidents similar to the ones you'll encounter during your career.

At the end of stage 2 training some forces will allow you to take a period of annual leave.

STAGE 3 (usually 2 weeks)

During stage 3 training you will start to prepare for stage 4, which is patrolling while under supervision of an experienced

officer. You will also learn about the priorities that are relevant to the specific area in which you'll be serving.

As you can imagine, each community has its own specific needs and requirements, and you will need to respond to these accordingly.

STAGE 4 – Patrolling experience with an experienced tutor (approximately 10 weeks)

This is where you get to put your knowledge into practice, under the close supervision of an experienced officer. It is during this stage of your training that you will really start to learn about the role of a police officer.

STAGE 5 (approximately 2 weeks)

After completion of patrolling you will be assessed to see how much you have learnt. This will then allow the police force to decide which areas, if any, you need to improve on. If you are good enough then you will be permitted to carry out independent patrol duties following further training relating to procedures and policies. If you are not quite ready for independent patrol then you will receive more training in specific areas.

STAGE 6 – Completion of your probation and further training

Once you are fully competent and ready for independent patrol you will be assigned to a Division where you will complete the remainder of your probationary training. You will also carry out further training in policies and procedures. Throughout this period you will be assessed continuously by your supervisory officers.

Opportunities for progression

If you are good at your job and you are a motivated and ambitious person then there will certainly be many opportunities for promotion within the force.

The Police Force will always need officers on the beat, but it also needs managers who are capable of driving the force forward in the direction it requires. Everyone in the Police Force has an equal opportunity for promotion, so if you are keen and enthusiastic, then there's nothing to stop you from reaching the top!

As you are probably aware, the Police Force also operates a High Potential Development Scheme. This scheme provides fast-track opportunities for those individuals who can demonstrate the right level of potential. The Police Force promotion scheme is open to everyone and is based upon merit. Work hard and you will be rewarded!

The working week

A normal working week for a police officer consists of 40 hours, which is usually divided up on a shift basis.

The shift pattern that you will normally work will form part of your contract and these do vary between each police force. All of the ranks below superintendent will be given two rest days every week and compensation will be given if you ever have to work during those two days.

If you need to know more about the different types of shift pattern you'll be required to work then you should contact your local constabulary.

Community Safety Partnerships

During my time in the Fire Service I sat on many different Community Safety Partnerships, or CSPs as they are otherwise called. In some areas these partnerships will be called an alternative name such as 'Crime and Disorder Reduction Partnerships'.

One of the main purposes of CSPs is for the local Police Force to meet up with other important organisations such as the Fire Service, Ambulance Service and the Local Authority

in order to discuss ways in which they can tackle crime collectively and make the community a safer place in which to live. There are Community Safety Partnerships for nearly every local authority area in England and Wales. Each one produces an audit and strategy for its local area.

Many partnerships look into community issues relating to their own particular area and some of those issues are concerned with the reduction of crime, anti-social behaviour, graffiti and fly-tipping to name but a few.

It is far easier for local authorities (councils) to improve community safety when they work in collaboration with other stakeholders such as the Fire and Rescue Services, Social Services, the Probation Service and CCTV working groups. For many years police forces and other stakeholders worked in isolation, until it was identified that more could be done if they worked with other relevant partners.

It is important to be aware that your work as a police officer may be as a direct result of requests from these partnerships. For example, there may be a problem with anti-social behaviour in a specific area of your county and you will be working hard to combat the problem.

Police community support officers

Police community support officers (PCSOs) do not have the same powers as a fully fledged police officer, yet they are a highly important part of crime prevention. They carry out visible patrolling within a specific area and are an effective crime deterrent, especially with regard to anti-social behaviour. Members of the public are more likely to provide PCSOs with important information relating to crime and anti-social behaviour as they spend more time in a specific area getting to know the community.

As well as being able to issue fixed penalty tickets for minor anti-social behaviour, PCSOs can also demand the name and address of a person acting in an anti-social manner. This

information can then be passed on to the police so that the relevant action can be taken. Other PCSO powers include being able to confiscate alcohol being consumed in a public place, confiscate tobacco from young people who are under age, and seize any vehicles that are being used to potentially harm other people, such as by joy-riders.

During your time within the force you will be required to work with PCSOs in your local area. It is important that you can work effectively with other members of the Police Force, both uniformed and non-uniformed, as part of a team in order to make the community a safer place to live.

Neighbourhood wardens

Neighbourhood wardens have been introduced by the Government to provide a highly visible, uniformed, semi-official presence in residential areas, town centres and high-crime areas. Unlike police community support officers, neighbourhood wardens do not have any police powers. They are designed to be the eyes and ears of the community, looking to improve the quality of life of a specific area within the community.

As a police officer, you will be working closely with neighbourhood wardens and also with members of the Neighbourhood Watch scheme, utilising their information to help reduce crime and anti-social behaviour in the area that you are responsible for.

We have now covered a number of important aspects of the police officer's role. Remember that the role is highly comprehensive and it involves a lot more than simply bringing offenders to justice. During your preparation you will need to visit the website of the Police Force you are applying to join and also read your recruitment literature to gain an in-depth knowledge of the force. If I was to ask you the question 'What can you tell me about the role of a police officer?' would you be able to answer it effectively?

Now let's move on to my top ten insider tips that will assist you during your preparation for becoming a police officer.

CHAPTER 3

THE TOP TEN INSIDER TIPS AND ADVICE

The following ten insider tips have been carefully put together to increase your chances of success during the police officer selection process. Therefore, it is important that you follow them carefully. While some of them will appear obvious they are still important tips which you need to follow.

1 Be fully prepared and focused

When you are applying for any career it is of vital importance that you prepare yourself fully for every stage of the selection process. What I mean is that you do everything you can to find out what is required of you. For example, most people do not read the guidance notes that accompany the application form, and then they wonder why they fail that particular section.

Make sure you read every bit of information you receive at least twice and understand what is required in order to pass. Things in life do not come easy and you must be prepared

to work hard. Go out of your way to prepare – for example, get a friend or relative to act out a role-play scenario and see how you deal with it. When completing the application form allocate plenty of time to do it neatly, concisely and correctly. Don't leave it until the night before the closing date to fill in the form as you will be setting yourself up to fail.

I will talk about 'preparation' on many occasions throughout this guide and I want you to take on board my advice.

Break down your preparation in the following four key areas:

Area 1 – Learn about the role of a police officer.

Area 2 – Learn and understand the core competencies.

Area 3 – Prepare to apply the core competencies to every stage of the selection process.

Area 4 – Improve your physical fitness.

In addition to your preparation strategy, it is also very important to believe in your own abilities and take advantage of the potential that's within you. If you work hard then you will be rewarded!

Whenever you come up against hurdles or difficult situations and experiences, always try to look for the opportunity to improve yourself. For example, if you have applied for the police previously and failed, what have you done to improve your chances of success the second time around? Did you find out what areas you failed on and have you done anything to improve?

2 Understand and believe in equality and fairness, and be able to demonstrate it during the selection process

Equality and fairness are crucial in today's society. We must treat each other with respect, dignity and understand that people come from backgrounds and cultures different from our own.

Treat people how you expect to be treated – with dignity and respect. If you do not believe in equality, fairness and dignity, then you are applying for the wrong job. Police officers are role models within society and people will look to you to set an example. For example, you wouldn't expect to see a police officer bullying or shouting at a member of the public in an aggressive manner would you? As a police officer you will use force only in exceptional circumstances. You will be required to use your interpersonal skills to diffuse situations and you will need to treat people fairly and equally at all times.

During the selection process your understanding and knowledge of equality and fairness issues will be tested on the application form, at the written tests and also during the interview and role-play scenarios. The core competency that relates to respect for race and diversity is the most important and you will not only have to learn it, but also believe in it.

There are many ways that you can prepare for this important core competency and within this guide I have provided you with a number of useful tips and advice that I recommend you spend time learning. Don't leave your success to chance. Make sure you understand exactly what equality and fairness and respect for race and diversity means and also what they stand for. More importantly, believe in them!

3 Be physically and mentally fit

Being prepared, both physically and mentally, is important if you are to succeed in your application to become a police officer. Even if you have only a few weeks to prepare, there are lots of ways in which you can improve your chances of success.

Many people who successfully pass the selection process are physically fit. Being physically fit has plenty of advantages in addition to simply improving your health. For example, raised self-esteem and confidence in your appearance are also benefits to keeping fit. A person with good health and

fitness generally shines when it comes to how they look, how they treat others, and how they go about their day-to-day activities.

In addition to the above, the benefits of 'fitness of mind' are equally as important when tackling the selection process. When applying to join the police you will be learning new skills and developing old ones. The fitter your mind, the easier this will be. If you are fit, both physically and mentally, then you will be able to prepare for longer. You will find that your stamina levels will increase and therefore your ability to practise and prepare will increase too.

Your free 'How to get police officer fit' guide provides you with a number of different exercises to choose from in order to prepare yourself for the fitness tests. A little bit each day will go a long way to helping you achieve your goal.

If you prepare yourself fully for the selection process then you will feel more confident on the day, when you are under pressure. Make sure you also get plenty of sleep in the build-up to selection and ensure you eat a healthy balanced diet.

Many of us underestimate the importance of a healthy diet. The saying 'we are what we eat' makes a lot of sense and you will find that if you just spend a week or two eating and drinking the right things you will begin to look and feel healthier. Avoid junk food, alcohol and cigarettes during your preparation and your concentration levels will increase greatly, helping you to get the most out of the work you put in.

Give yourself every opportunity to succeed!

4 Learn about the Police Force you are applying to join

This is important for a number of reasons. To begin with, you may be asked a question on the application form that relates to your knowledge of the role of a police officer and also why you want to join that particular force. As you can appreciate, many candidates will apply for a number of different forces

all at once in an attempt to secure a job as a police officer. The Police Force you are applying to join wants to know what exactly attracts you to it. In order to be able to provide a good response to this type of question, you will need to carry out some research.

The second reason is that some police forces are now holding 'final interviews', which are in addition to the standard competency based assessment centre interview. During this interview it is guaranteed that you will be asked questions relating to your knowledge of the force.

Most police forces have a website. Visit their website and find out what they are doing in terms of community policing. Remember that the job of a police officer is not just about catching criminals. It is about delivering the best possible service to the public and responding to their needs. Understanding what the police in your area are trying to achieve will demonstrate enthusiasm, commitment and an understanding of what your job will involve if you are successful.

If you can tell the interview panel about the policing area, current crime trends and statistics, community policing issues and even diversity recruitment, then you will be displaying a far greater knowledge of their force and also showing them that you have made the effort! Also make sure that you are aware of the 'Policing Pledge'.

If you were interviewing a candidate for employment in your Police Force, what would you expect them to know about your organisation? You would probably expect them to know a great deal of information. Learn as much information as possible about the force you are applying to join and be extremely thorough in your preparation.

The easiest way to find out about your local force is to visit the Police Could You? website at www.policecouldyou.co.uk. Here you will find contact details and links to the website of your chosen force.

5 Learn and understand the core competencies

VERY IMPORTANT – DO NOT IGNORE

The police officer core competencies form the fundamental requirements of the role. They identify how you should perform and they are key to the role of a police officer. Read them carefully and make sure you understand them, as they are crucial to your success!

Throughout the selection process you should concentrate on the core competencies, constantly trying to demonstrate them at every stage.

When completing the application form your answers should be based around the core competencies. The same rule applies to the written tests, the interview and also the role-play exercises. The most effective way to achieve this is to use 'keywords and phrases' in your responses to the application form and interview questions. You can also adopt this method when tackling the role-plays and the written tests. Using keywords and phrases that correspond to the core competencies will gain you higher scores. Within this guide I will show you how to achieve this, but the first step is for you to learn the core competencies.

Make sure you have a copy of the competencies next to you when completing the application form and while preparing for the assessment centre.

The core competencies cover a wide range of required skills and attributes including team working, customer focus, problem solving and equality and fairness issues, to name but a few.

This is the most important tip I can provide you with – Do not ignore it!

6 Be patient and learn from your mistakes

We can all become impatient when we really want something in life but sometimes it may take us a little longer than expected to reach our goals.

Try to understand that the Police Force receives many thousands of applications each year and it takes time for them to process each one. Don't contact the Police Force with a view to chasing up your application but rather wait for them to get in touch with you. Use the time in between your results wisely, concentrating on the next stage of the selection process. For example, as soon as you submit your application form, start working on your preparation for the assessment centre; 99 per cent of candidates will not start their preparation for the assessment centre until they receive their results. They can't be bothered to prepare for the next stage until they receive conformation that they've been successful, and as a result, they are missing out on a few extra weeks' practice time.

During the police officer courses that I teach (see p. x) I am amazed at how many students have their assessment the following week. They sometimes inform me that they have done no preparation since prior to the course and this always baffles me. Remember that you are applying to join a job that will pay you a salary of approximately £30,000 a year! That to me is worth studying very hard for. So, use every bit of spare time you get wisely by not sitting around in between results but rather using that time to prepare for the next stage.

Once again, while teaching students, I am always left amazed at how many of them have previously failed selection, yet done nothing to find out why they failed and in particular which areas they need to improve on. If you have previously been through selection then it is crucial that you find out why you failed. This will allow you to improve for next time. You should receive a feedback form from the Police Force

informing you which areas you need to improve on. It is pointless going through selection again unless you improve on your weak areas, as you will simply make the same mistakes again.

7 Understand diversity and the benefits it brings to a workforce and society

A diverse community has great benefits and the same can be said for a diverse workforce.

The Police Force is no exception and it needs to represent the community in which it serves. If society itself is multi-cultural, then the Police Force needs to be too, if it is to provide the best possible service to the community in which it serves.

Ask yourself the question 'What is diversity?' If you cannot answer it then you need to find out. You will almost certainly be asked a question about it during the application form stage and the final interview, if applicable.

The Police Force must uphold the law fairly and appropriately to protect, respect, help and reassure everyone in all communities. The Police Force must also meet all of the current legislative requirements concerning human rights, race, disability and all employment law that relates to equality.

The focus of the Police Force is to provide a service that responds to the needs of all communities, ensuring the promotion of fair working practices at all times. The concept of diversity encompasses acceptance and respect. It means understanding that each individual is unique, and recognising our individual differences. These can be along the dimensions of race, ethnicity, gender, sexual orientation, socio-economic status, age, physical abilities, religious beliefs, political beliefs, or other ideologies. It is about understanding each other and moving beyond simple tolerance to embracing and celebrating the rich dimensions of diversity contained within each individual.

Learn, understand and believe in diversity. It is important during the selection process and even more important in relation to your role as a police officer.

8 Do not give up until you have reached your goal

If you don't reach the required standard at the first or subsequent attempts, don't give up. So long as you always try to better yourself, there is always the chance that you will succeed. If you do fail any of the stages look at the area(s) you need to improve on.

Did you fail the fitness test? If so then there are ways of improving. Don't just sit back and wait for the next opportunity to come along, prepare for it straight away and you'll increase your chances for next time.

Many people give up on their goals far too easily. Learning to find the positive aspects of negative situations is a difficult thing to do but a skill that anyone can acquire through practice and determination.

If you really want to achieve your goals then anything is possible.

During your preparation set yourself small targets each week. For example, your first week may be used to concentrate on learning the core competencies. Your second week can be used to prepare for your written responses on the application form and so on.

If you get tired or feel de-motivated at any time during your preparation, walk away from it and give yourself a break. You may find that you come back to it re-energised, more focused and determined to succeed!

9 Practise the role-play exercises with a friend or relative

The role-play scenarios can be a daunting experience, especially if you've never done anything like this before. While

the Police Force will advise you to be yourself, there are ways in which you can prepare and subsequently increase your chances of success.

The way to prepare for the role-plays is to act them out in a room with a friend or relative. Within this guide you have been provided with a number of example role-play scenarios. Use these to practise with, and hone your skills in each area of the core competencies that are being assessed.

The only way that you will be able to understand what is required during the role-play exercises is to learn the assessable core competencies. For example, if you are being assessed against the core competency of customer focus, then you will need to demonstrate the following during each role-play scenario:

- Be professional and present an appropriate image in line with your brief and job description.

- Focus on the needs of the customer in every scenario.

- Sort out any problems as soon as possible and apologise for any errors or mistakes that have been made.

- Ask the customer whether they are satisfied with your actions or not. If they are not, then take alternative steps to make them satisfied if possible.

- Keep the customer updated on progress.

Doing all of the above, in addition to covering the other assessable areas, can be quite a difficult task. However, if you practise these skills regularly in the build-up to your assessment then you will find it becomes easier and easier the more that you do.

10 Practise a mock interview

Mock interviews are a fantastic way to prepare for both the assessment centre interview, and also the final interview, if applicable.

During the build up to interviews in the past, I would write down a number of predicted interview questions that I had created during my research. I would then ask a friend or relative to ask me these questions under formal interview conditions. I found this to be excellent preparation and it certainly served me well during all of my career interviews. I would estimate that I was successful at over 90 per cent of all interviews I attended. I put down this success purely to this form of preparation.

I would also strongly recommend that you sit down on a chair in front of a long mirror and respond to the same set of interview questions. Watch your interview technique. Do you slouch? Do you fidget and do you overuse your hands?

It is important that you work on your interview technique during the build up to the assessment centre and the final interview.

Do not make the mistake of carrying out little or no preparation, because you can be guaranteed that some of the other candidates will have prepared fully. Make sure you put in the time and effort and practise a number of mock interviews. You will be amazed at how confident you feel during the real interview.

Bonus tip – Consider carrying out some community work

Demonstrating that you are capable of working effectively in the community before you join the police will give you a positive edge over other candidates. Being able to add this information to your application and also at the interview stage will make you stand out from the rest of the competition.

Why not organise a small charity event in your local area? Maybe a sponsored swim, cycle ride or car wash? The reason why I advise undertaking this type of project is that it gives you more relevant experiences to draw on during the selection process.

If you organise such an event on your own or as a team then it demonstrates your ability to organise and solve problems, which are key police officer core competencies. It also demonstrates that you are a caring person and that you are prepared to go out of your way to help others. You may also get fit in the process!

Other effective ways of working in the community are either through Neighbourhood Watch schemes, becoming a special constable, part-time firefighter or carrying out any form of voluntary work. Make the effort and go out on a limb to stand out from the rest of the applicants.

Now that we have taken a look at the top insider tips and advice, let us now put all that we have learnt so far into practice. The first step is the successful completion of the application form.

HOW TO COMPLETE THE APPLICATION FORM

CHAPTER 4
POLICE OFFICER CORE COMPETENCIES

The application form is the first stage of the selection process for becoming a police officer. During this section I will provide you with a step-by-step approach to completing a successful application. It is important to point out that I have used a number of the more common types of application form questions within this section and it is your responsibility to confirm that they relate to your particular form. I have deliberately not made reference to any sections of the form that relate to personal details, simply because what you write here is based on you and you alone.

Whenever I have completed application forms in the past I have always set aside plenty of time to do them justice. I would recommend you allow at least five evenings to complete the form, breaking it up into manageable sections. Many candidates will try to complete the form in one sitting and, as a result, their concentration will wane and so will the quality of their submission.

You will be asked a number of questions on the application form, and on the following pages I have provided you with some tips and advice on how to approach these questions. Please remember that these are provided as a guide only and you should base your answers around your own experiences in both work life and personal life. Questions that are based around 'knowledge, skills and experience' are looking for you to demonstrate that you can meet the requirements of the 'person specification' for the job you are applying for. Therefore, your answer should match these as closely as possible.

Your first step is to find out what the 'person specification' is for the particular force you are applying to join. Essentially, the role of a police officer is made up of a number of core competencies. You may receive these in your application pack or alternatively they can usually be found on the Police Could You? website, or on the website of the force you are applying to join. Whatever you do, make sure you get a copy of them, and have them by your side when completing the application form. Basically you are looking to match your responses with the police officer core competencies.

Once you have found the 'core competencies', now is the time to structure your answer around these, ensuring that you briefly cover each area based upon your own experiences in both your work life and personal life.

The core competencies that form the basis of the police officer role are similar to the following. Please note that the core competencies can, and do, change from time to time so it is important to confirm that they are correct.

Respect for race and diversity

This essentially involves considering and showing respect for the opinions, circumstances and feelings of colleagues and members of the public, no matter what their race, religion, position, background, circumstances, status or appearance.

We have already touched on this important subject and you will no doubt be aware of how important it is to the role of a police officer.

Team working

Police officers must be able to work in teams as well as having an ability to work on their own, unsupervised. In order to meet this core competency you will need to be able to develop strong working relationships both inside and outside the team. If there are barriers between different groups then you will need to have the skills to break them down and involve other people in discussions and decisions that you make.

Community and customer focus

As a police officer you must focus on the customer. The customer is essentially any members of the public whom you will be dealing with. You will need to be capable of providing a high-quality service that is tailored to meet each person's individual needs. Throughout the selection process you will be assessed on this area and we have already looked at this core competency in relation to the role-play exercises described in insider tip number 9.

The only way that you can provide a high-quality service to the public is by understanding the needs of your community. Once you understand the needs of your community then you will be able to provide an excellent service.

Effective communication

Police officers must be able to communicate both verbally and in writing. You will also need to communicate to the people you are addressing in a style and manner that is appropriate. This can sometimes be difficult but with practice, it can be achieved.

As a serving police officer you will be required to take accurate notes of incidents that you attend. Therefore the Police Force that are applying to join will want to assess your potential in this area during the written tests element of the selection process.

Problem solving

In order to solve problems effectively you will first need to gather sufficient information. This can usually be achieved through a number of sources. For example, if as a police officer you were investigating a burglary, you would first want to gather witness statements from the owner of the property and also the owners of surrounding properties. This information may then lead to other information sources, which will allow you to gather sufficient evidence to make decisions that will ultimately lead to the problem being solved through effective decision making.

Personal responsibility

Police officers have a reputation for getting things done. They are very good at taking personal responsibility for making things happen and achieving results. In order to effectively achieve this you will need to display a level of motivation, commitment, perseverance and conscientiousness. At all times you will need to act with a high degree of integrity.

Resilience

As a police officer you will do doubt be faced with difficult and pressurised circumstances. It is during these tough situations that you will need to show resilience. For example, imagine turning up to a 999 call where a number of drunken lads are refusing to leave a pub after closing time. How would you deal with the situation? You must be prepared to make difficult decisions and have the confidence to see them through.

Important Tips

Now that we have taken a brief look at the core competencies, we can start to look at some of the application form questions. But before we do this, read the following important tips, which will help you to submit a first-class application.

- Make sure you read the whole of the application form at least twice before preparing your responses, including the guidance notes.

- Read and understand the person specification and the police officer core competencies.

- Try to tailor your answers around the 'core competencies' and include any keywords or phrases you think are relevant.

- Make sure you base your answers on actual events that you have experienced either in your work life or personal life.

- Fill out the form in the correct ink colour. If you fail to follow this simple instruction then your form may end up in the bin!

- If there is a specific word count for each question, make sure you stick to it.

- Make sure you keep a photocopy of your completed application form before sending it off as you could be asked questions relating to it during the interview stage if you progress that far.

- Do not lie.

- Get someone to read your practice/completed application form to check for spelling/grammar mistakes. You lose marks for poor grammar/spelling.

- Finally, send your application form recorded delivery. This will prevent your form going missing in the post, which happens more often than you think.

CHAPTER 5
SAMPLE APPLICATION FORM QUESTIONS AND RESPONSES

The following sample application form questions may not be applicable to your specific form. However, they will provide you with some excellent tips and advice on how to approach the questions.

Core competency based questions

Sample question 1

What knowledge, skills and experiences do you have that will enable you to meet the requirements of a police officer?

ANSWER (example only)

In my previous employment as a customer services assistant I was required to work closely with the general public on many occasions. Often I would be required to provide varied solutions to customers' problems or complaints after listening

to their concerns. It was always important for me to listen carefully to what they had to say and respond in a manner that was both respectful and understanding.

On some occasions I would have to communicate with members of the public from a different race or background and I made sure I paid particular attention to making sure they understood how I was going to resolve their problems for them. I would always be sensitive to how they may have been feeling on the other end of the telephone.

Every Monday morning the team that I was a part of would hold a meeting to discuss ways in which we could improve our service to the customer. During these meetings I would always ensure that I contributed and shared any relevant experiences I had had during the previous week. Sometimes during the group discussions I would find that some members of the group were shy and not very confident at coming forward, so I always sensitively tried to involve them wherever possible.

I remember on one occasion during a meeting I provided a solution to a problem that had been ongoing for some time. I had noticed that customers would often call back to see if their complaint had been resolved, which was often time consuming for the company to deal with. So I suggested that we should have a system where customers were called back after 48 hours with an update of progress in relation to their complaint. My suggestion was taken forward and is now an integral part of the company's procedures. I found it quite hard at first to persuade managers to take on my idea but I was confident that the change would provide a better service to the customers.

First of all read the example answer I have provided above. Then try to 'match' the answer to the core competencies that are relevant to the role of a police officer and you will begin to understand what is required.

For example, the first paragraph reads as follows:

In my previous employment as a customer services assistant I was required to work closely with the general public on many occasions. Often I would be required to provide varied solutions to customers' problems or complaints after listening to their concerns. It was always important for me to listen carefully to what they had to say and respond in a manner that was both respectful and understanding.

The above paragraph matches elements of the core competency of community and customer focus.

Now take a look at the next paragraph:

On some occasions I would have to communicate with members of the public from a different race or background and I made sure I paid particular attention to making sure they understood how I was going to resolve their problems. I would always be sensitive to how they may have been feeling on the other end of the telephone.

The response matches elements of the core competency of respect for race and diversity.

Hopefully you are now beginning to understand what is required and how important it is to 'match' your response with the core competencies that are being assessed. Remember to make sure you read fully the guidance notes that are contained within your application pack. I hope you will also start to realise why I recommend you set aside five evenings to complete the form!

It is also possible to use examples from your personal life, so don't just think about work experiences but look at other aspects of your life too. Try also to think of any community work that you have been involved in. Have you been a special constable or do you work for a charity or other similar organisation? Maybe you are a member of Neighbourhood Watch and if so you should find it quite a simple process to match the core competencies.

ry to tailor your responses to the core competencies that are being assessed and briefly cover each assessable area if possible. You may also want to include keywords and phrases from the core competencies when constructing your response.

Below, I have provided a number of sample keywords and phrases that are relevant to each core competency. These will help you to understand exactly what I mean when I say 'match' the core competencies in each of your responses.

Keywords and phrases to consider using in your responses to the application form questions

Respect for race and diversity

- Show respect for others
- Take into account the feelings of colleagues

Team working

- Develop strong working relationships
- Achieve common goals
- Break down barriers
- Involve others

Community and customer focus

- Focusing on the customer
- High-quality service
- The needs of others
- Understand the community
- Commitment

Effective communication

- Communicates ideas
- Effective communication
- Understand others

Problem solving

- Gather information
- Analyse information
- Identify problems
- Make effective decisions

Personal responsibility

- Take personal responsibility
- Achieve results
- Motivation
- Commitment
- Perseverance
- Conscientiousness
- Act with a high degree of integrity

Resilience

- Make difficult decisions
- Confidence

Now let's move on to some more sample application form questions and responses.

Sample question 2

Why have you applied for this post and what do you have to offer?

Some Police Force application forms may ask you questions based around the question above. If so, then you need to answer again in conjunction with the 'person spec' relevant to that particular force.

An example answer for the above question could be based around the following:

I believe my personal qualities and attributes would make me suitable for employment as a police officer within this Constabulary. I enjoy working in a diverse organisation that offers many and varied challenges. I would enjoy the challenge of working in a customer-focused environment that requires a high level of personal responsibility, openness to change and teamwork. I have a high level of commitment, motivation and integrity, which I believe would help the Police Force respond to the needs of the community.

Top Tips

- The length of response that you provide should be dictated by the amount of space available to you on the application form or the specified number of maximum words.

- The form itself may provide you with the facility to attach a separate sheet if necessary. If it doesn't then make sure you keep to the space provided.

- The best tip I can give you is to write down your answer first in rough before committing your answer to paper on the actual application form. This will allow you to iron out any mistakes.

Sample question 3

It is essential that police officers are capable of showing respect for other people regardless of their background. Please describe a situation when you have challenged someone's behaviour that was bullying, discriminatory or insensitive. You will be assessed on how positively you acted during the situation, and also on how well you understood what had occurred.

PART 1 – Describe the situation and also tell us about the other person or people who were involved.

While working as a salesperson for my previous employer, I was serving a lady who was from an ethnic background. I was helping her to choose a gift for her son's seventh birthday when a group of four youths entered the shop and began looking around at the goods we had for sale.

For some strange reason they began to make racist jokes and comments to the lady. I was naturally offended by the comments and was concerned for the lady to whom these comments were directed.

Any form of bullying and harassment is not welcome in any situation and I was determined to stop it immediately and protect the lady from any more harm.

> **Top Tips**
>
> - Try to answer this type of question focusing on the positive action that you took, identifying that you understood the situation. Don't forget to include keywords and phrases in your response that are relevant to the competencies that are being assessed.
>
> - Make sure you are honest in your responses. The situations you provide MUST be real and ones that you took part in.

PART 2 – What did you say and what did you do?

The lady was clearly upset by their actions and I too found them both offensive and insensitive. I decided to take immediate action and stood between the lady and the youths to try to protect her from any more verbal abuse or comments. I told them in a calm manner that their comments were not welcome and would not be tolerated. I then called over my manager for assistance and asked him to call the police before asking the four youths to leave the shop.

I wanted to defuse the situation as soon as possible, being constantly aware of the lady's feelings. I was confident that the shop's CCTV cameras would have picked up the four offending youths and that the police would be able to deal with the situation.

After the youths had left the shop I sat the lady down and made her a cup of tea while we waited for the police to arrive. I did everything that I could to support and comfort the lady and told her that I would be prepared to act as a witness to the bullying and harassment that I had just witnessed.

Top Tip

Remember to read the core competencies before constructing your response. What are the police looking for in relation to what you say to others and how you act?

PART 3 – Why do you think the other people behaved as they did?

I believe it is predominantly down to a lack of understanding, education and awareness. Unless people are educated and understand why these comments are not acceptable then they are not open to change.

They behave in this manner because they are unaware of how dangerous their comments and actions are. They believe it is socially acceptable to act this way when it certainly isn't.

Top Tip

When describing your thoughts or opinions on how others acted in a given situation, keep your personal views separate. Try to provide a response that shows a mature understanding of the situation.

PART 4 – What would have been the consequences if you had not acted as you did?

The consequences are numerous. To begin with I would have been condoning this type of behaviour and missing an opportunity to let the offenders know that their actions are wrong (educating them). I would have also been letting the lady down, which would have in turn made her feel frightened, hurt and not supported.

We all have the opportunity to help stop discriminatory behaviour and, providing we ourselves are not in any physical danger, then we should take positive action to stop it.

Top Tip

Try to demonstrate an understanding of what would have possibly happened if you had failed to take action.

Sample question 4

Police officers are required to work in teams and therefore they must be able to work well with others. Please describe a situation when it was necessary to work with other people in order to get something done

and achieve a positive result. During this question you will be assessed on how you co-operated with the other members of the team in completing the task in hand.

PART 1 – Tell us what had to be done.

While driving along the motorway I noticed that an accident had just occurred up in front of me. Two cars were involved in the accident and some people in the car appeared to be injured. There were a number of people standing around looking at the crash and I was concerned that help had not been called.

We needed to work as a team to call the emergency services, look after the injured people in the cars and try to stay as safe as possible.

Top Tip

Make sure you provide a response to the questions that is specific in nature. Do not fall into the trap of telling them what you 'would do' if the situation was to occur.

PART 2 – How was it that you became involved?

I became involved through pure instinct. I'm not the type of person to sit in the background and let others resolve situations. I prefer to help out where I can and I believed that, in this situation, something needed to be done. It was apparent that people were hurt and the emergency services had not been called yet.

There were plenty of people around but they weren't working as a team to get the essentials done.

> **Top Tip**
>
> It is better to say that you volunteered to get involved rather than that you were asked.

PART 3 – What did you do and what did others do?

I immediately shouted out loud and asked if anybody was a trained first aid person, nurse or doctor. A man came running over and told me that he worked for the British Red Cross and that he had a first aid kit in his car. He told me that he would look after the injured people but that he would need an assistant. I asked a lady if she would help him and she said that she would. I then decided that I needed to call the emergency services and went to use my mobile phone.

A man pointed out to me that if I used the orange emergency phone I would get through quicker and the operator would be able to locate exactly where the accident was. I asked him if he would call the emergency services on the orange phone, as he appeared to know exactly what he was doing. I noticed a lady sitting on the embankment next to the hard shoulder crying and she appeared to be a bit shocked.

I asked an onlooker if he would mind sitting with her and talking to her until the ambulance got there. I thought this was important so that she felt supported and not alone.

Once that was done, the remaining onlookers and I decided to work as a team to remove the debris lying in the road, which would hinder the route for the oncoming emergency service vehicles.

> **Top Tip**
>
> Provide a response that is both concise and flows in a logical sequence.

PART 4 – How was it decided how things were going to be done?

I decided to take the initiative and get everyone working as a team. I asked the people to let me know what their particular strengths were. One person was first aid trained and so he had the task of attending to the injured. Everyone agreed that we needed to work together as a team in order to achieve the task.

PART 5 – What did you do to ensure the team members were able to get the result they wanted?

I took control of a deteriorating situation and got everybody who was standing around doing nothing involved. I made sure I asked if anybody was skilled in certain areas such as first aid and used the people who had experience, such as the man who knew about the orange emergency telephones.

I also kept talking to everybody and asking them if they were OK and happy with what they were doing. I tried my best to co-ordinate the people who had jobs that I felt needed to be done as a priority.

> **Top Tip**
>
> Try to include details that demonstrate how your actions had a positive impact on the result.

PART 6 – What benefit did you see for yourself in what you did?

The benefit overall was for the injured people, ensuring that they received treatment as soon as possible. However, I did feel a sense of achievement that the team members had worked well together even though we had never met each other before. I also learnt a tremendous amount from the experience.

At the end we all shook hands and talked briefly, and there was a common sense of achievement among everybody that we had done something positive. Without each other we wouldn't have been able to get the job done.

> **Top Tip**
>
> Try to explain that the benefit was positive.

Sample question 5

During very difficult circumstances, police officers must be able to remain calm and act logically and decisively. Please describe a situation when you have been in a very challenging or difficult situation and had to make a decision where other people disagreed with you. You will be assessed in this question on how positively you reacted in the face of adversity and challenge.

PART 1 – Tell us about the situation and why you felt it was difficult.

While working in my current position as a salesperson I was the duty manager for the day as my manager had gone sick. It was the week before Christmas and the shop was very busy.

During the day the fire alarm went off and I started to ask everybody to evacuate the shop, which is our company policy. The alarm has gone off in the past but the normal manager usually lets people stay in the shop while he finds out if it's a false alarm.

This was a difficult situation because the shop was very busy, nobody wanted to leave and my shop assistants were disagreeing with me in my decision to evacuate the shop. Some of the customers were becoming irate as they were in the changing rooms at the time.

> **Top Tip**
>
> For questions of this nature you will need to focus on the core competency that relates to resilience. Remember to use keywords and phrases in your responses that match the core competencies being assessed.

PART 2 – Who disagreed with you and what did they say or do?

Both the customers and my shop assistants were disagreeing with me. The customers were saying that it was appalling that they had to evacuate the shop and that they would complain to the head office about it.

The sales staff were trying to persuade me to keep everybody inside the shop, saying that it was most probably a false alarm as usual. I was determined to evacuate everybody from the shop for safety reasons and would not allow anybody to deter me from my aim.

The safety of my staff and customers was at the forefront of my mind even though it wasn't at theirs.

> **Top Tip**
>
> Do not become aggressive or confrontational when dealing with people who disagree with you. Remain calm at all times but be resilient in your actions if it is right to do so.

PART 3 – What did you say or do?

While remaining calm and in control I shouted at the top of my voice that everybody was to leave, even though the sound of the alarm was reducing the impact of my voice. I then had to instruct my staff to walk around the shop and tell everybody to leave while we investigated the problem.

I had to inform one member of staff that disciplinary action would be taken against him if he did not co-operate. Eventually, after I kept persisting, everybody began to leave the shop. I then went outside with my members of staff, took a roll call and waited for the Fire Brigade to arrive.

Top Tip

Remember to be in control at all times and remain calm. These are qualities that good police officers will possess.

PART 4 – Tell us how this situation made you feel initially.

At first I felt a little apprehensive and under pressure but determined not to move from my position as I knew 100 per cent that it was the right one. I was disappointed that my staff did not initially help me but the more I persisted the more confident I became.

This was the first time I had been the manager of the shop so I felt that this situation tested my courage and determination. By remaining calm I was able to deal with the situation far more effectively.

Top Tips

- Do not say that you felt angry and do not use words that are confrontational.

- By staying calm you will be able to deal with situations far more effectively.

PART 5 – How did you feel immediately after the incident?

I felt good because I had achieved my aim and I had stood by my decision. It made me feel confident that I could do it again and deal with any difficult situation. I now felt

that I had the courage to manage the shop better and had proven to myself that I was capable of dealing with difficult situations.

I had learnt that staying calm under pressure improves your chances of a successful outcome dramatically.

Sample question 6

Police officers must deliver an excellent service to the public. It is also important that they build good working relationships with the public and other stakeholders. Describe a situation when you had to deal with someone who was disappointed with the level of service they received. Try to use an occasion where you had contact with that person over a period of time or on a number of different occasions in order to rectify the problem.

PART 1 – Describe the situation and why you think the person was not happy.

While working as a salesperson in my current job, I was approached by an unhappy customer. He explained to me, in an angry manner, that he had bought a pair of running trainers for his daughter's birthday the week before. When she unwrapped her present on the morning of her birthday she noticed that one of the training shoes was a size 6 while the other one was a size 7.

Understandably, he was not happy with the level of service that he had received from our company. The reason for his dissatisfaction was that his daughter had been let down on her birthday and, as a consequence, he then had to travel back into town to sort out a problem that should not have occurred in the first place.

> **Top Tips**
>
> - In order to respond to this type of question accurately you will need to study and understand the core competency that relates to customer focus.
>
> - Make sure you answer the question in two parts. Describe the situation and then explain why the person was not happy.

PART 2 – Explain what you did in response to his concerns.

Immediately I tried to defuse his anger by telling him that I fully understood his situation and that I would feel exactly the same if I was in his position. I promised him that I would resolve the situation and offered him a cup of tea or coffee while he waited for me to address the problem. This appeared to have the effect of calming him down and the tone in his voice became friendlier.

I then spoke to my manager and explained the situation to him. I suggested that maybe it would be a good idea to replace the running shoes with a new pair (both the same size) and also refund the gentleman in full as a gesture to try to make up for our mistake. The manager agreed to my suggestion and so I returned to the gentleman concerned and explained what we proposed to do for him. He was delighted with the good will offer and appeared to calm down totally.

We then went over to the checkout to refund his payment and replace the running shoes. At this point I took down the gentleman's address and telephone number, which is company policy for any goods returned for refund or exchange. The man then left the shop happy with the service he had received.

The following day I telephoned the gentleman at home to check that everything was all right with the running shoes and he told me that his daughter was delighted. He also informed me that despite the initial bad experience he would still use our shop in the future.

Top Tip

Remember that customer focus is an important element of the role of a police officer. You must focus on the needs of the customer at all times.

PART 3 – How did you know that the person was happy with what you did?

I could detect a change in his behaviour as soon as I explained that I sympathised with his situation. Again, when I offered him a cup of tea or coffee I detected a change in his behaviour once more.

The tone in his voice became less agitated and angry so I took advantage of this situation and tried even harder to turn his bad experience with us into a positive one. When we offered him the refund along with the replacement of the running shoes his attitude changed again but this time he appeared to be satisfied.

Finally, when I telephoned him the following day he was so happy that he said he would come back to us again despite the initial poor level of service.

Top Tip

In your response to this part of the question try to indicate that you followed up your actions by contacting the person to see if they were satisfied with what you did for them.

PART 4 – If you hadn't acted like you did what do you think the outcome would have been?

To begin with I believe the situation would have become even more heated and possibly untenable. His anger or dissatisfaction could have escalated if my attempts to defuse the situation had not taken place. I also believe that we would have lost a customer and, therefore, lost future profits and custom for the company. There would have been a high possibility that the gentleman would have taken his complaint higher, either to our head office, trading standards or the local newspaper.

Customer service is important and we need to do everything we can (within reason) to make the level of service we provide as high as possible. I also believe that our reputation could have been damaged as that particular gentleman could have told friends or colleagues not to use our shop in the future, whereas now, he is maybe more inclined to promote us in a positive light instead.

Top Tip

- Demonstrate that you have a clear understanding of what would have happened if you had not acted as you did.

- Study the core competency that is relevant to customer focus before answering this question.

- Use keywords and phrases in your response from the core competency that is being assessed.

Sample question 7

Police officers must be organised and manage their own time effectively. Please describe a situation when you were under pressure to carry out a number of tasks at the same time.

Tell us what you had to do, which things were a priority and why.

While working for a sales company as a manager I had four important tasks to complete on the last working day of every month. These tasks included stocktaking reports, approving and submitting the sales reps' mileage claims, auditing the previous month's accounts and planning the strategy for the following month's activity.

My first priority was always to approve and submit the sales reps' mileage claims. If I did not get this right or failed to get them submitted on time the reps would be out of pocket when they received their payslip. This would in turn affect morale and productivity within the office. The second task to complete would be the stocktaking reports.

This was important to complete on time as if I missed the deadline we would not have sufficient stock for the following month, and therefore there would be nothing to sell and customers would not receive their goods on time. The third task would be the strategy for the following month. This was usually a simple task but still important as it would set out my plan for the following month's activities.

Finally, I would audit the accounts. The reason why I would leave this task until the end is that they did not have to be submitted to Head Office until the 14th day of the month and therefore I had extra time to complete this task and ensure that I got it right the first time.

Top Tip

Try to demonstrate that you have excellent organisation skills and that you can cope with the demands and pressures of the job.

Sample question 8

Police officers must be capable of communicating effectively with lots of different people, both verbally and in writing.

Please explain a situation when you had to tell an individual or a group of people something that they may have found difficult or distressing. You will be assessed on how well you delivered the message and also on what you took into account when speaking to them.

PART 1 – Who were the people and what did you have to tell them?

The people involved were my elderly nextdoor neighbours. They had a cat that they had looked after for years and they were very fond of it. I had to inform them that their cat had just been run over by a car in the road.

PART 2 – Why do you think they may have found the message difficult or distressing?

I was fully aware of how much they loved their cat and I could understand that the message I was about to tell them would have been deeply distressing. They had cherished the cat for years and to suddenly lose it would have been a great shock to them.

PART 3 – How did you deliver the message?

To begin with I knocked at their door and asked calmly if I could come in to speak to them. Before I broke the news to them I made them a cup of tea and sat them down in a quiet room away from any distractions. I then carefully and sensitively told them that their cat had passed away following an accident in the road. At all times I took into account their feelings and I made sure I delivered the message sensitively and in a caring manner.

PART 4 – Before you delivered your message, what did you take into account?

I took into account where and when I was going to deliver the message. It was important to tell them in a quiet room away from any distractions so that they could grieve in peace. I also took into account the tone in which I delivered the message and made sure that I was sensitive to their feelings. I also ensured that I would be available to support them after I had broken the news.

Top Tips

- Read the question carefully and make sure you answer every element of it.

- Read the core competency that is relevant to effective communication before providing a response to this question.

You may find on the application form that some of the questions are based around different core competencies. If this is the case then simply apply the same process of trying to match the core competencies by using keywords and phrases in your responses.

Questions based around your reasons and motivations for wanting to become a police officer

In addition to the standard core competency based questions, you may be asked additional questions that are centred around your motivations for wanting to become a police officer with this particular Police Force.

On the following pages I have provided a number of different questions and sample responses to assist you. Please remember that the responses provided here, and in other parts of this book, are for guidance purposes only. The responses

you provide on your application form must be based around your own individual circumstances and beliefs.

Sample question I

How long have you been thinking about becoming a police officer and what has attracted your attention to the role?

I have been considering a career as a police officer ever since I started my current job as a sales manager, approximately seven years ago. I enjoy working in a customer-focused environment and thrive on providing high levels of service to customers. I have always been aware that the police officer's role is demanding, hard work and highly challenging, but the rewards of such a job are what attracted my attention in the first place.

The opportunity to work as part of an efficient team and work towards providing the community with an effective service would be highly rewarding and satisfying.

Top Tips

- It is not advisable to state that you have become interested only recently. Candidates who have been seriously thinking about the job for a while will potentially score higher marks.

- Try to demonstrate in your response that you have studied the role carefully and that you believe your skills are suited to being a police officer.

- Those candidates who state that they are attracted solely to the 'catching criminals' side of the role will not score highly.

- Read the core competencies and the job description carefully before responding to this question.

- Never be critical of a previous employer.

Sample question 2

What have you done to prepare for this application?

I have carried out a great deal of research to ascertain whether I am suitable for the role of a police officer and also to find out whether this career would satisfy my career aspirations. I have studied in depth the police officer core competencies to ensure that I can meet the expectations of this Police Force. I have also carried out extensive research before applying to this particular Police Force as opposed to just applying to any force and hoping that I get in.

My research began on the internet through the official police service websites, before finally studying this particular force's website. I have also spoken to current serving police officers at my local station to ask about the role of a working police officer and how it affects their social life.

Finally, I have discussed my intentions with my immediate family to ensure that I have their full support and encouragement.

Top Tip

You will recall at the beginning of this guide how much emphasis I placed on preparation leading to success. The police want to know how much preparation you have done and also the type of preparation. If you have carried out plenty of in-depth and meaningful preparation then it demonstrates to them that you are very serious about wanting this job. Those applicants who carry out little or no preparation may be simply 'going through the motions'.

Tips for Completing a Successful Application Form

While some of the following tips have already been provided within this chapter, it is important that we provide them again. Your success very much depends on your ability to do the following:

- Read the application form and the guidance notes at least twice before you complete it.

- If possible, photocopy the application form and complete a draft copy first. This will allow you to make any errors or mistakes without being penalised.

- Obtain a copy of the core competencies and have them at your side when completing the form.

- Take your time when completing the form and set aside plenty of time for each question. I recommend that you spend five evenings completing the application form, breaking it down into manageable portions. This will allow you to maintain high levels of concentration.

- Complete the form in the correct colour ink and follow all instructions very carefully. Your form could be thrown out for simply failing to follow simple instructions.

- Be honest when completing the form and if you are unsure about anything contact the Police Force for confirmation.

- Try not to make any spelling or grammar errors. You WILL lose marks for poor spelling, grammar and punctuation.

- Try to use keywords and phrases in your responses to the assessable questions that are relevant to the core competencies.

- Get someone to check over your form for errors before you submit it. If they can't read your application form, the assessor probably won't be able to either.

(Continued)

(Continued)

- Take a photocopy of your final completed form before submitting it.

- Try to submit the form well before the closing date. Some forces may operate a cut-off point in terms of the number of applications they receive.

- Some forms do get lost in the post so it is advisable that you send it by recorded delivery for peace of mind.

- If your form is unsuccessful ask for feedback, if available. It is important that you learn from your mistakes.

What happens after you have sent off your application form?

Once you have completed and sent off your application form there will be a waiting period before you find out whether or not you have been successful. Some forces will write to you only if you have been successful.

Regardless of the above, it is crucial that you start preparing for the assessment centre even before you receive your result. By starting your preparation early you will effectively be giving yourself a two-to-three-week advantage over the other applicants; 99 per cent of applicants will wait to receive their result before they start to prepare. This is where you can gain an advantage.

In the next section you will learn about the assessment centre and the different stages that you may have to go through. Prepare fully for each stage and really go out of your way to improve your skills and knowledge of the selection process.

Please note that the information you are about to read may differ from force to force. Make sure you confirm the exact requirements of your particular assessment centre before you start preparing.

NATIONAL RECRUITMENT
ASSESSMENT CENTRE

CHAPTER 6
HOW TO PREPARE FOR THE ASSESSMENT CENTRE

Once you have successfully passed the application form stage of the process you will be invited to attend an assessment centre. The assessment centre location will vary from force to force but you will be provided with details, times and location. Make sure you know exactly where your venue is and don't be late.

The assessment centre is designed to assess your suitability for recruitment into the Police Force. The assessment is usually conducted over a period of five hours but this may vary from force to force.

For the assessment centre you will be required to take a number of important documents with you to confirm your identity to the police. The forms of identification can vary but the more usual types include:

- a full ten-year passport or TWO of the following:

- British driving licence

- P45

- full birth certificate

- cheque book and bank card with three statements and proof of signature

- identify or membership card containing a photograph of yourself

- proof of residence (e.g. council tax, gas, electricity, water or telephone bill).

Make sure that you read the information given to you and take along the relevant documents because if you do not, you won't be able to continue with the assessment procedure. At the assessment centre you will be required to undertake a numerical reasoning test, a verbal reasoning test, written exercises, interactive/role-play exercises and a competency based structured interview. Some police forces now require you to sit a final interview which normally comes after the assessment.

In the numerical reasoning test you may be asked to answer multiple-choice questions that will assess your ability to solve numerical problems accurately. In the verbal logical reasoning test you will be asked to answer multiple-choice questions that will measure your ability to reason logically when given facts about events which are similar to the type that a police officer is required to deal with. In the written and interactive exercises, you may have to assume the role of a newly appointed customer services officer at a fictitious retail and leisure complex. You will note that the title 'customer services officer' is very similar to the role of a police officer in as much as you will be dealing with members of the public.

During the interview you may be asked questions about how you have dealt with situations in your past and I have provided in-depth information to help you pass this stage in the next section of this guide.

Prior to attending the assessment centre you will be provided with an information pack, which you must read and familiarise yourself with all of its content.

When preparing to complete the application form you will have already learnt a considerable amount of job specific information that is relevant to the role of a police officer. Once again, the core competencies are going to form the basis of your preparation and you should have a copy of them next to you when preparing for each stage of the assessment centre.

In relation to the written tests preparation, only you will know your current skill level and will therefore need to decide how much time you allocate to this area. The majority of candidates are not overly concerned about the numerical and verbal reasoning tests but they are when it comes to report writing. Within this guide you will receive some invaluable advice relating to every area of assessment so make sure you read it carefully and try to answer the sample test questions.

The role-play exercises can be a daunting experience. However, if you practise them beforehand, and learn how to demonstrate the core competencies being assessed, then your confidence will increase dramatically. A thorough explanation of how to prepare for them has been provided within this guide. Once again, centre your role-play preparation around the core competencies, as this is how the police will assess you.

In addition to the assessment centre interview, many police forces have introduced a 'final interview' as I have already mentioned. The reason for this additional interview is so that the Police Force can assess you in addition to the competency based structured interview which involves set questions. The assessment centre interview focuses purely on the core competencies and, providing you put in the work, it is relatively easy to pass. Within this guide I have provided you with detailed information on how to prepare for both types of interview. It is important that you check with the

Police Force you are applying to join whether or not you will be required to sit a final interview.

In the following three chapters I will break down each assessment centre area in detail to allow you to prepare effectively.

CHAPTER 7

THE WRITTEN TESTS

When preparing for the numerical and verbal reasoning tests, the most effective way to increase your scores is simply to practise answering plenty of sample questions. Within this section I have provided you with a number of sample test questions. In addition to these you may also decide to purchase additional testing resources. If you do decide to pursue this option then I recommend the following:

- Numerical reasoning and verbal reasoning testing booklets from the website www.how2become.co.uk.

- Consider practising online tests through the website www. job-test.co.uk.

Below, I have provided a number of practice sample questions that you may encounter during your tests. It is unlikely that you will be asked these exact questions during your assessment, but please do use them as part of your preparation.

Verbal reasoning questions 1–8

Work as quickly as possible through each question and see how well you score. Try to understand each question and read it carefully. The answers to each question are at the end of the exercises.

Use a pen and paper, and answer each question as **True**, **False** or **Impossible to say**.

REMEMBER TO ANSWER YOUR QUESTIONS BASED SOLELY ON THE INFORMATION GIVEN AND NOT ON YOUR OWN OPINIONS OR VIEWS.

Verbal reasoning question 1

A fire has occurred in a nightclub belonging to Harry James. One person died in the fire, which occurred at 11p.m. on Saturday night. The club was insured for less than its value.

True, False or Impossible to say?

1. The fire occurred at 1100 hours.

2. A relative of Harry James was killed in the fire.

3. If the insurance company decides to pay out for the fire, Harry James stands to make a profit.

4. The fire was caused by arson.

5. The club was not insured at the time of the fire.

Verbal reasoning question 2

An accident occurred on the M6 motorway between junctions 8 and 9 southbound at 3p.m. The driver of a Ford Fiesta was seen to pull into the middle lane without indicating, forcing another car to veer into the central reservation. One person suffered a broken arm and was taken to hospital before the police arrived.

True, False or Impossible to say?

1. The accident was on the M6 motorway on the carriageway that leads to Scotland.

2. The driver of the Ford Fiesta was injured in the crash.

3. The central reservation was responsible for the accident.

4. The police did not give first aid at the scene.

5. The accident happened at 1500 hours.

Verbal reasoning question 3

A man of between 30 and 35 years of age was seen stealing a car from outside Mrs Brown's house yesterday. He was seen breaking the nearside rear window with a hammer before driving off at 40 miles per hour. He narrowly missed a young mother who was pushing a pram.

True, False or Impossible to say?

1. The man who stole the car was 34 years old.

2. He stole Mrs Brown's car.

3. The young mother who was pushing a pram was injured.

4. He used a hammer to smash the windscreen.

5. When he drove off he was breaking the speed limit.

Verbal reasoning question 4

A shopkeeper called Mr Smith was seen serving alcohol to a girl aged 16.

The girl had shown him fake ID, which was a driving licence belonging to her sister. The incident occurred at around 11.30p.m. on a Wednesday evening during December.

True, False or Impossible to say?

1. The girl is old enough to purchase alcohol from Mr Smith.

2. The girl purchased the alcohol for her sister.

3. The girl's sister had given the driving licence to her.

4. Mr Smith will receive a custodial sentence for his actions.

Verbal reasoning question 5

Following a bank robbery in a town centre, six masked gunmen were seen speeding away from the scene in a black van. The incident, which happened in broad daylight in front of hundreds of shoppers, was picked up by CCTV cameras. Police are appealing for witnesses. The local newspaper has offered a £5,000 reward for any information leading to the conviction of all the people involved.

True, False or Impossible to say?

1. The car in which the gunmen drove off was a black van.

2. Someone must have seen something.

3. The incident was picked up by CCTV cameras.

4. The newspaper will pay £5,000 for information leading to the arrest of all of the men involved.

5. Police are not appealing to members of the public for help.

Verbal reasoning question 6

A factory fire at 'Stevenage Supplies' was arson, the police have confirmed. A man was seen running away from the scene shortly before the fire started. Earlier that day a man was sacked from the company for allegedly stealing money

from the safe. The incident is the second one to occur at the factory in as many months.

True, False or Impossible to say?

1. Police have confirmed that the fire at the factory was arson.

2. The man who was seen running away from the fire was the man who started it.

3. One previous 'fire-related' incident has already occurred at the factory.

4. The man who was sacked from the factory may have started the fire.

Verbal reasoning question 7

At 1800 hours today police issued a statement in relation to the crime scene in Armstrong Road. Police have been examining the scene all day and reports suggest that it may be murder. Forensic officers have been visiting the incident and inform us that the whole street has been cordoned off and nobody will be allowed through. Police say that the street involved will be closed for another 18 hours and no access will be available to anyone during this time.

True, False or Impossible to say?

1. Police have confirmed the incident is murder.

2. Forensic officers have now left the scene.

3. The road will be open at 12 noon the following day.

4. Although the street has been cordoned off, taxis and buses will be given access.

5. Forensic officers will be at the scene all night.

Verbal reasoning question 8

Mrs Rogers telephoned the police at 8p.m. to report a burglary at her house in Gamble Crescent. She reports that she came home from work and her front bedroom window was open but she doesn't remember leaving it open.

She informs the police that her jewellery box is missing and also £40 cash, which was left on the kitchen table. She came home from work at 5p.m. and left again at 7a.m. No other signs of forced entry were visible.

True, False or Impossible to say?

1. The burglar made his/her way in through the bedroom window.

2. The burglar took the jewellery and £40 cash before leaving.

3. Mrs Rogers was away from the house for 10 hours in total.

4. Mrs Rogers may have left the window open herself before leaving for work.

5. There were other visible signs of forced entry.

Answers to verbal reasoning questions 1–8

Question 1	Question 2
1. False	1. False
2. Impossible to say	2. Impossible to say
3. False	3. False
4. Impossible to say	4. True
5. False	5. True

Question 3

1. Impossible to say

2. Impossible to say

3. False

4. False

5. Impossible to say

Question 4

1. False

2. Impossible to say

3. Impossible to say

4. Impossible to say

Question 5

1. True

2. Impossible to say

3. True

4. False

5. False

Question 6

1. True

2. Impossible to say

3. True

4. True

Question 7

1. False

2. Impossible to say

3. True

4. False

5. Impossible to say

Question 8

1. Impossible to say

2. Impossible to say

3. False

4. True

5. False

Now that you have had the chance to try out a number of verbal reasoning test questions, hopefully you are beginning to grasp what is required. It is very easy to get caught out when answering these types of questions due to the fact that you have to rely solely on the information provided, something that is integral to the role of a police officer.

Now try the next set of sample verbal reasoning questions.

Verbal reasoning questions 9–12

Verbal reasoning question 9

The local bank was held up at gunpoint on Monday, 18 September, at approximately 4p.m. The thieves used a black motorcycle to make their getaway. The following facts are also known about the incident:

- Two shots were fired.
- There were 12 staff members on duty at the time of the raid.
- The alarm was raised by the manager and the police were called.
- The cashier was ordered to hand over a bag of money containing £7,000.
- The thieves have not yet been caught.
- Police are appealing for witnesses.

True, False or Impossible to say?

1. The thieves have been caught.
2. The cashier raised the alarm.
3. The cashier was shot.
4. Two people were injured.
5. The bank was open for business at the time of the incident.

Verbal reasoning question 10

A father and son were found dead in their two-bedroom flat in Sparsbrook on Sunday evening. They had both been suffocated. The following facts are also known:

- The victims were identified by the police as Mark Webster, 16 years old, and his father, Thomas Webster, 39 years old.

- Thomas was in debt to the sum of £37,000.

- Two men were seen leaving the house at 4p.m. on Sunday afternoon.

- Two men were seen acting suspiciously in the area on Saturday evening before driving off in a brown Ford Escort car.

- Thomas had previously contacted the police to express his concerns about his safety following threats from his creditors.

- The house had not been broken into.

True, False or Impossible to say?

1. The people Thomas owed money to could have been responsible for the deaths.

2. The two men seen leaving the house were not responsible for the deaths of Mark Webster and Thomas Webster.

3. The house had been broken into.

4. Neighbours reported two men acting suspiciously in the area on Saturday evening.

5. The people responsible for the deaths drove off in a brown Ford Escort car.

Verbal reasoning question II

Firefighters have discovered a large quantity of cannabis during a fire on a farm in the village of Teynsville. Police have cordoned off the area. The following facts are also known about the incident:

- The farm is owned by local farmer Peter Watts.

- The fire was started deliberately.

- Peter Watts has two previous convictions for possession and supply of Class A drugs.

- Peter Watts' wife was at home on the night of the fire.

- Peter Watts was visiting friends in the nearby town of Grentshill when the fire started.

- A passer-by reported the fire to the police at 9p.m.

- Peter Watts has been arrested on suspicion of possession of cannabis.

True, False or Impossible to say?

1. Cannabis is a Class A drug.

2. The fire was started accidentally.

3. A passer-by reported the fire to the Fire Service at 9p.m.

4. The cannabis found during the fire belonged to Peter Watts.

5. Peter Watts has been arrested for possession of cannabis.

Verbal reasoning question 12

A row of terraced houses was partly destroyed by an explosion on 17 April 2007. Just before the explosion a man was seen running back into his house. He had reported a gas leak to the national gas emergency services seven days prior to the explosion. The following facts are also known about the incident:

- The smell of gas had also been reported by two other residents in the weeks leading up to the explosion.

- The police are investigating possible terrorist connections with one of the residents.

True, False or Impossible to say?

1. A gas leak was reported to the national gas emergency services on 10 April 2007.

2. The explosion was caused by a gas leak.

3. The explosion was not caused by a terrorist attack.

4. The man seen running back into his house had already reported a gas leak to the national gas emergency services.

5. The row of terraced houses that was involved in the explosion has been damaged.

Answers to verbal reasoning questions 9–12

Question 9
1. False
2. False
3. Impossible to say
4. Impossible to say
5. Impossible to say

Question 10
1. True
2. Impossible to say
3. False
4. Impossible to say
5. Impossible to say

Question 11
1. Impossible to say
2. False
3. False
4. Impossible to say
5. False

Question 12
1. True
2. Impossible to say
3. Impossible to say
4. True
5. True

Tips for passing the verbal reasoning test

- In the build-up to the assessment, make sure you practise answering plenty of sample test questions. Little and often is far more effective than cramming the night before your assessment.

- Read the questions carefully. During the test you may have to answer questions that are answered either TRUE, FALSE, or IMPOSSIBLE TO SAY. Base your answers on the evidence supplied only and not on your own views or opinions.

(Continued)

(Continued)

- Do not spend too long on one particular question. If you cannot answer it then move on to the next question, but make sure you leave a space on the answer sheet.

- Consider purchasing additional verbal reasoning test booklets or practice aids. You can obtain these through the website www.how2become.co.uk.

- Get plenty of sleep the night before the test. This will allow you to concentrate fully.

Numerical reasoning tests

As part of the written tests you may also have to sit a numeracy assessment.

The most effective way to prepare for this type of test is to practise answering sample numerical reasoning tests.

Apart from these sample questions, there are a number of alternative methods for improving your scores. You may wish to invest in a psychometric numerical reasoning test booklet so that you can practise more tests. You can obtain more sample tests through the website www.how2become. co.uk. The more you practise the better you will become at answering these types of questions.

Remember – practice makes perfect!

Below, I have provided a number of sample numeracy tests to help you prepare. Try to answer the questions quickly and without the use of a calculator. You have five minutes in which to answer the 14 questions.

Numerical reasoning questions – exercise 1

1. A wallet has been found containing one £20 note, five £5 notes, a 50 pence coin and three 2 pence coins. How much is in the wallet?

Answer

2. Subtract 200 from 500, add 80, subtract 30 and multiply by 2. What number do you have?

Answer

3. A multi-storey car park has 8 floors and can hold 72 cars on each floor. In addition to this there is also allocation for 4 disabled parking spaces per floor. How many spaces are there in the entire car park?

Answer

4. A man saves £12.50 per month. How much would he have saved after one year?

Answer

5. If there have been 60 accidents along one stretch of a motorway in the last year, how many on average have occurred each month?

Answer

6. Out of 40,000 applicants only 4,000 are likely to be successful. What percentage will fail?

Answer

7. What percentage of 400 is 100?

Answer

8. Malcolm's shift commences at 0615 hours. If his shift is 10.5 hours long what time will he finish?

Answer

9. If Mary can bake 12 cakes in 2 hours how many will she bake in 10 hours?

Answer

10. If there are 24 hours in the day how many hours are there in one week?

Answer

11. Susan has 10 coins and gives 5 of them to Steven and the remainder to Alan. Alan gives 3 of his coins to Steven who in turn gives half of his back to Susan. How many is Susan left with?

Answer

12. Add 121 to 54. Now subtract 75 and multiply by 10. What is the result?

Answer

13. Ahmed leaves for work at 8a.m. and arrives at work at 9.17a.m. He then leaves work at 4.57p.m. and arrives back at home at 6.03p.m. How many minutes has Ahmed spent travelling?

Answer

14. A car travels at 30 km/h for the first hour, 65 km/h for the second hour, 44 km/h for the third hour and 50 km/h for the fourth hour. What is the car's average speed over the four-hour journey?

Answer

Answers to numerical reasoning questions – exercise

1. £45.56
2. 700
3. 608
4. £150
5. 5
6. 90%
7. 25%
8. 1645 hours or 4.45p.m.
9. 60 cakes
10. 168
11. 4
12. 1000
13. 143 minutes
14. 47.25 km/h

Now that you have had a chance to work through exercise 1, try answering the questions in exercise 2. Don't forget to work quickly yet accurately.

Numerical reasoning questions – exercise 2

You are not permitted to use a calculator during this exercise.

There are 20 multiple-choice questions and you have 10 minutes in which to answer them all.

1. Your friends tell you their electricity bill has gone up from £40 per month to £47 per month. How much extra are they now paying per year?

   a. £84   **b.** £85   **c.** £83   **d.** £86   **e.** £82

   Answer

2. A woman earns a salary of £32,000 per year. How much would she earn in 15 years?

   a. £280,000   **b.** £380,000   **c.** £480,000
   d. £260,000   **e.** £460,000

   Answer

3. If a police officer walks the beat for 6 hours at a pace of 4 km/h, how much ground will she have covered after the 6 hours is over?

a. 20 km   **b.** 21 km   **c.** 22 km   **d.** 23 km   **e.** 24 km

Answer

4. It takes Malcolm 45 minutes to walk 6 miles to work. At what pace does he walk?

a. 7 m.p.h   **b.** 4 m.p.h   **c.** 6 m.p.h   **d.** 5 m.p.h
e. 8 m.p.h

Answer

5. Ellie spends 3 hours on the phone talking to her friend abroad. If the call costs 12 pence per 5 minutes, how much does the call cost in total?

a. £3.30   **b.** £4.32   **c.** £3.32   **d.** £4.44   **e.** £3.44

Answer

6. A woman spends £27 in a retail store. She has a discount voucher that reduces the total cost to £21.60. How much discount does the voucher give her?

a. 5%   **b.** 10%   **c.** 15%   **d.** 20%   **e.** 25%

Answer

7. A group of seven men spends £21.70 on a round of drinks. How much does each of them pay if the bill is split evenly?

a. £3.00   **b.** £65.10   **c.** £3.10   **d.** £3.15   **e.** £3.20

Answer

8. 45,600 people attend a football match to watch Manchester United play Tottenham Hotspur. If there are 32,705 Manchester United supporters at the game, how many Tottenham Hotspur supporters are there?

a. 12,985   **b.** 13,985   **c.** 12,895   **d.** 12,895   **e.** 14,985

Answer

9. The police are called to attend a motorway accident involving a coach full of passengers. A total of 54 people are on board, 17 of whom are injured. How many are not injured?

a. 40   **b.** 39   **c.** 38   **d.** 37   **e.** 36

Answer

10. A car journey usually takes 6 hours and 55 minutes, but on one occasion the car stops for a total of 47 minutes. How long does the journey take on this occasion?

a. 6 hrs 40 mins   **b.** 5 hrs 45 mins   **c.** 7 hrs 40 mins
d. 7 hrs 42 mins   **e.** 6 hrs 42 mins

Answer

11. There are 10 people in a team. Five of them weigh 70 kg each and the remaining five weigh 75 kg each. What is the average weight of the team?

a. 72.5 kg   **b.** 71.5 kg   **c.** 70.5 kg   **d.** 72 kg   **e.** 71 kg

Answer

12. A kitchen floor takes 80 tiles to cover. A man buys 10 boxes, each containing 6 tiles. How many more boxes does he need to complete the job?

a. 2 boxes   b. 4 boxes   c. 6 boxes   d. 8 boxes
e. 10 boxes

Answer

13. How much money does it cost to buy 12 packets of crisps at 47 pence each?

a. £6.45   b. £5.64   c. £6.54   d. £4.65   e. £5.46

Answer

14. A motorcyclist is travelling at 78 m.p.h on a road where the speed limit is 50 m.p.h. How much over the speed limit is he?

a. 20 m.p.h   b. 22 m.p.h   c. 26 m.p.h
d. 28 m.p.h   e. 30 m.p.h

Answer

15. A removal firm loads 34 boxes onto a van. If there are 27 boxes still to be loaded, how many boxes are there in total?

a. 49   b. 50   c. 61   d. 52   e. 53

Answer

16. When paying a bill at the bank you give the cashier one £20 note, two £5 notes, four £1 coins, six 10p coins and two 2p coins. How much have you given him?

a. £34.64   b. £43.46   c. £34.46   d. £63.44
e. £36.46

Answer

17. If you pay £97.70 per month on your council tax bill, how much would you pay quarterly?

a. £293.30 **b.** £293.20 **c.** £293.10 **d.** £293.00
e. £292.90

Answer

18. Four people eat a meal at a restaurant. The total bill comes to £44.80. How much do they need to pay each?

a. £10.00 **b.** £10.10 **c.** £10.20 **d.** £11.10
e. £11.20

Answer

19. A worker is required to work for 8 hours a day. He is entitled to three 20-minute breaks and one 1-hour lunch break during that 8-hour period. If he works for 5 days per week, how many hours will he have worked after 4 weeks?

a. 12 hours **b.** 14 hours **c.** 120 hours
d. 140 hours **e.** 150 hours

Answer

20. If there are 1610 metres in a mile, how many metres are there in 4 miles?

a. 640 **b.** 6040 **c.** 6044 **d.** 6440 **e.** 644

Answer

Answers to numerical reasoning questions – exercise 2

1. **a.** £84

In this question you need to first work out the difference in their electricity bill. Subtract £40 from £47 to be left with £7. Now you need to calculate how much extra they are paying per year. If there are 12 months in a year then you need to multiply £7 by 12 months to reach your answer of £84.

2. c. £480,000

The lady earns £32,000 per year. To work out how much she earns in 15 years, you must multiply £32,000 by 15 years to reach your answer of £480,000.

3. e. 24 km

To work out this answer all you need to do is multiply the 6 hours by the 4 km/h to reach the total of 24 km. Remember that she is walking at a pace of 4 km/h for a total of 6 hours.

4. e. 8 m.p.h

Malcolm walks 6 miles in 45 minutes, which means he is walking 2 miles every 15 minutes. Therefore, he would walk 8 miles in 60 minutes (1 hour), so he is walking at 8 m.p.h.

5. b. £4.32

If the call costs 12 pence for every 5 minutes then all you need to do is calculate how many 5 minutes there are in the 3-hour telephone call. There are 60 minutes in every hour, so therefore there are 180 minutes in 3 hours. 180 minutes divided by 5 minutes will give you 36. To get your answer, just multiply 36 by 12 pence to reach your answer of £4.32

6. d. 20%

This type of question can be tricky, especially when you don't have a calculator! The best way to work out the answer is to first of all work out how much 10% discount would give you off the total price. If £27 is the total price, then 10% would be a £2.70 discount. In monetary terms the woman has received £5.40 in discount. If 10% is a £2.70 discount then 20% is a £5.40 discount.

7. c. £3.10

Divide £21.70 by 7 to reach your answer of £3.10.

8. d. 12,895

Subtract 32,705 from 45,600 to reach your answer of 12,895.

9. d. 37

Subtract 17 from 54 to reach your answer of 37.

10. d. 7 hrs 42 minutes

Add the 47 minutes to the normal journey time of 6 hours and 55 minutes to reach your answer of 7 hours and 42 minutes.

11. a. 72.5 kg

To calculate the average weight, you first need to add each weight together. Therefore, (5 × 70) + (5 × 75) = 725 kg. To find the average weight you must now divide the 725 by 10, which will give you the answer 72.5 kg.

12. b. 4 boxes

The man has 10 boxes, each of which contains 6 tiles. He therefore has a total of 60 tiles. He now needs a further 20 tiles to cover the total floor area. If there are 6 tiles in a box then he will need a further 4 boxes (24 tiles).

13. b. £5.64

Multiply 12 by 47 pence to reach your answer of £5.64.

14. d. 28 m.p.h

Subtract 50 m.p.h from 78 m.p.h to reach your answer of 28 m.p.h.

15. c. 61

Add 34 to 27 to reach your answer of 61 boxes.

16. a. £34.64

Add all of the currency together to reach the answer of £34.64.

17. c. £293.10

To reach the answer you must multiply £97.70 by 3. Remember, a quarter is every 3 months.

18. e. £11.20

Divide £44.80 by 4 people to reach your answer of £11.20.

19. c. 120 hours

First, you need to determine how many 'real' hours he works each day. Subtract the total sum of breaks from 8 hours to reach 6 hours per day. If he works 5 days per week then he is working a total of 30 hours per week. Multiply 30 hours by 4 weeks to reach your answer of 120 hours.

20. d. 6440 metres

Multiply 1610 metres by 4 to reach your answer of 6440 metres.

Tips for Passing the Numerical Reasoning Test

- Answer plenty of sample test questions in the build-up to the assessment.

- Work without a calculator. This will increase your skill at being able to answer the questions.

- Work quickly yet accurately through the test. If you miss a question then make sure you leave a gap on the answer sheet.

- If you generally struggle with this type of test then consider getting a personal tutor.

- During the test do not concentrate on the other candidates and how fast they are working. Keep your head down and focus only on your own performance.

CHAPTER 8

THE WRITTEN EXERCISES – REPORT AND LETTER WRITING

While you are at the assessment centre you may be asked to undertake two written exercises. The written exercise may be in the form of a report, letter, memo or proposal.

When you create a written report, the assessor is looking for a well-structured piece of writing that is logical and relevant. You should demonstrate a good use and understanding of English grammar and not make too many spelling mistakes (a maximum of ten), but your aim should be to make zero errors.

The written report is an area of the police officer assessment process that many people think they do not need to practise. They use their preparation time before their assessment date predominantly looking at the role-plays and the interview. Important as they both are, the written report can gain you the highest percentage of marks out of the three written tests. This could mean the difference between a pass and a fail.

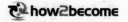

On the assessment day, you will be allowed 20 minutes to read all of the information provided and create your report. This is not a lot of time, especially if you are not prepared. Therefore, it is important that you work fast and accurately. In this chapter I will show you how to manage this time, so you can gather all the relevant information and put it together in a well-structured and logical report.

During the written assessment you may have to assume the role of a customer services officer of a fictitious retail centre. The report you are asked to create will be for the centre manager, or someone similar, based around a specific theme. When you are sent the details of your assessment date, you will also be sent two information packs – Information to Candidates and the Centre Welcome Pack (this is the fictitious centre in which you are a customer services officer). Before I move on to a sample question and, in particular, how to answer it, I am going to provide you with some very important tips on how to prepare and also how to pass the report writing exercise.

Important Tips

- You must learn the contents of the welcome pack before you attend the assessment centre. This will make your life a lot easier during each assessment, including the report writing element. If you don't know what your role involves before you attend the assessment centre then you are going to spend a lot of your time learning it during the actual tests! Learn it inside out *before* you go.

- As I have constantly stressed throughout this guide, learn the core competencies before you go to assessment centre. Memorise keywords and phrases so that you can easily match them during each stage of the assessment.

- In the build-up to the assessment centre practise the sample written report exercises that I have provided in this guide. The more you practise, the better you will become.

- Improve your handwriting so that it is neat and easy to read. Make the assessor's life as easy as possible. Try to imagine that the person scoring your report may have been marking forms for weeks on end! If they come across yours and it is easy to read, concise and it flows in a logical sequence, they are far more likely to pass it.

- During the assessment use only words that you can spell. If you are unsure about a word, do not use it.

Below is an example of the type of exercise you could be given.

Sample written report exercise 1

You are the customer services officer for a retail centre. Your manager has asked you to compile a report based on a new pub that is being opened in the centre. Your manager is meeting with the pub owners in a few days' time to discuss several issues and he wants you to write a report based on the information provided. The pub owners have requested that the pub is open to serve alcoholic beverages from 11a.m. until 11p.m.

Below are the results of a survey, which tell you that, on the whole, the general public and staff are not happy with the idea of a pub being opened in the shopping centre because of perceived anti-social behavioural problems, littering and rowdiness.

It is your job to create a report for your manager stating what the main issues are and what your recommendations would be.

Survey results for sample exercise 1

The following information has been taken from a survey that was conducted among 100 members of public who regularly shop at the centre and 30 employees who work at the centre.

- 60 per cent of the general public and 80 per cent of employees felt that the opening of a pub in the centre would increase littering.

- 80 per cent of the general public and 60 per cent of employees thought that rowdiness in the centre would increase as a result of the pub opening.

- 10 per cent of the general public and 10 per cent of employees thought that the opening of the pub would be a good idea.

Below is an example of how the report could be written. There are many different recommendations that could have been made.

You should consider the information you have gathered and make the recommendation(s) you consider to be the best for those circumstances.

Remember: recommendations are suggestions for actions or changes. They should be specific rather than general. It is important that you answer the question and state what are your main findings and recommendations.

Sample response to written report exercise 1

> From: The Customer Services Officer
> To: The Centre Manager
> Subject: New pub
>
> Sir,
>
> Please find detailed my findings and recommendations in relation to the new pub, as requested. The survey conducted took into consideration the views and opinions of 100 members of the public and 30 members of staff who work at the centre.

While a small proportion of staff and public (10 per cent) felt that the opening of the pub would be a good idea, the majority of people surveyed felt that there would be problems with anti-social behaviour, littering and rowdiness.

Having taken into consideration all of the information provided, I wish to make the following recommendations:

The level of customer service that the centre currently provides is high and it is important that this is maintained. It is important to take into consideration the views and opinions of our customers and staff and to see things from their point of view. I believe that there would be a high risk involved if we were to allow the pub to serve alcoholic beverages from 11a.m. until 11p.m. and that problems with anti-social behaviour could develop. We have a responsibility to protect the public and to ensure that they are safe while in the centre.

While it is important initially to obtain the views of the pub owners, I recommend that the pub is permitted to serve alcoholic beverages only from 11a.m. until 1p.m. and from 5p.m. until 7p.m. so as to reduce the risk of the above problems developing.

I have recommended this course of action, as I believe it is in the best interests of the centre, its staff and more importantly our valued customers. This alternative course of action would be for a trial period only and providing there are no problems with anti-social behaviour, littering or rowdiness we could look to review the opening hours with a view to extending them. I am prepared to take full responsibility for monitoring the situation once the pub has been opened. I will keep you updated on progress.

Customer Services Officer

Now that you have read the sample response, look at the following five-step approach that I use when creating a well-structured report.

How to create an effective report – the five-step approach

Step 1

Read the information provided in the exercise quickly and accurately

Remember that you only have 20 minutes in which to create your report. Therefore, you do not want to spend too long reading the information. I would suggest that you spend two to three minutes maximum reading the information.

Step 2

Extract relevant information from irrelevant information (main findings)

When you read the information provided in the exercise you will notice that some of the information is of no significance. Write down which information is relevant in brief details only – these should be your main findings.

Step 3

Decide what recommendations you are going to suggest or what action(s) you are going to take

One of the police officer core competencies is that of problem solving. If asked to, then you must come up with suitable recommendations. Do not 'sit on the fence', but rather provide a logical solution to the problem.

Step 4

Construct your report in a logical and concise manner
You are being assessed on your ability to communicate effectively.
Therefore you must construct your report in a logical and concise
manner. You must also ensure that you answer the question.

Step 5

**Include keywords and phrases from the core competencies in
your report**
During each report or letter that you construct I strongly
advise that you include keywords and phrases from the core
competencies.

You will notice that the five-step approach is easy to follow.
Therefore, I strongly suggest that you learn it and use
it during the practice exercises provided later on in this
section.

To begin with, let's go back to the sample response that
I provided to the first exercise and I will explain how to
implement the five-step approach. Step 1 requires you to
read the information quickly and accurately. Because you
will have already learnt the Welcome Pack you will be aware
of your responsibilities under it, and you will also be aware
of the fact that you must be able to provide a high level of
service.

Step 2 requires you to extract relevant information from
irrelevant information. In order to demonstrate what is relevant
I have underlined the key points.

Sample written report exercise 1

<u>You are the customer services officer</u> for a retail centre. Your manager has asked you to compile a report based on a <u>new pub that is being opened in the centre</u>. Your manager is meeting with the pub owners in a few days' time to discuss several issues and he wants you to write a report based on the information provided. <u>The pub owners have requested that the pub is open to serve alcoholic beverages from 11 a.m. until 11 p.m</u>.

Below are the results of a survey, which tell you that, on the whole, <u>the general public and staff are not happy with the idea of a pub being opened in the shopping centre</u> because of perceived anti-social behavioural problems, littering and rowdiness.

It is your job to create a report for your manager <u>stating what the main issues are</u> and what <u>your recommendations would be</u>.

Survey results for sample exercise 1

The following information has been taken from a survey that was conducted among 100 members of the public who regularly shop at the centre and 30 employees who work at the centre.

- 60 per cent of the general public and 80 per cent of employees felt that the opening of a pub in the centre would increase littering.

- 80 per cent of the general public and 60 per cent of employees thought that rowdiness in the centre would increase as a result of the pub opening.

- 10 per cent of the general public and 10 per cent of employees thought that the opening of the pub would be a good idea.

So, why are the key points that I underlined relevant? Allow me to explain:

<u>You are the customer services officer</u>
Because you will have already read the Welcome Pack prior to attending the assessment centre and, in particular, your duties and responsibilities within it, you will have noticed that it is your job to provide a high level of service. Therefore, the report that you create needs to cater for everyone's needs. In relation to this particular situation you must provide a solution that caters for the needs of the pub owners, the centre and also the members of public and employees.

<u>new pub that is being opened in the centre.</u>
The information you have been provided with tells you clearly that a new pub is opening in the centre. Therefore, the pub needs to operate as a business and by doing so it needs to serve alcoholic beverages. Despite the fact that the majority of people surveyed are against the pub opening, the pub still needs to function as a business. Bear this in mind when detailing your recommendations.

<u>The pub owners have requested that the pub is open to serve alcoholic beverages from 11a.m. until 11p.m.</u>
The pub owners have quite rightly requested that the pub opens from 11a.m. until 11p.m. and serves alcoholic beverages during this period. However, you still need to provide a high level of service to everyone. Therefore, you may decide to recommend a reduced opening time for a trial period only. Always look for the obvious solution to the problem.

<u>the general public and staff are not happy with the idea of a pub being opened in the shopping centre</u>
Because the general public and staff are not happy with the idea of a pub opening in the centre you will need to take this into account when constructing your response.

<u>stating what the main issues are</u>
Your first task when writing your report is to do just that – state what the main issues are.

<u>your recommendations would be</u>
Once you have detailed the main issues you will then need to make your recommendations, which should be based on sound judgement and common sense.

During step 3 you will need to come up with your recommendations. Remember that as a police officer you will need to solve problems based on the information and facts provided. In this particular case I have decided to offer a solution that meets the needs of all parties concerned – reduced opening times for a trial period with a view to extending them if all goes well. When creating your report do not be afraid to come up with sensible recommendations or solutions.

During step 4 you will create your report. It is important that your report is concise, relevant and that it flows in a logical sequence. I would strongly recommend that you construct it using the following format:

Beginning

During the introduction provide brief details as to what the report is about. You should also provide brief details that relate to your findings. In this particular question I am being asked to detail the main issues and my recommendations. Therefore, I will detail the main issues during the beginning section of the report.

Middle

Here you will write your main findings and recommendations. Remember to include keywords and phrases that you have learnt from the core competencies.

End

This is the summary and conclusion. Say why you have recommended this course of action. Are there any further

recommendations? If you are expecting there to be feedback, explain how you propose to deal with this. You may also wish to state that you will take full responsibility for seeing any action through and for keeping your manager updated on progress.

In order to demonstrate how effective the beginning, middle and end method can be I have boxed off each section of the sample response to written exercise 1 below.

Creating a report using a beginning, middle and an end

Sir,

Please find detailed my findings and recommendations in relation to the new pub, as requested. The survey conducted took into consideration the views and opinions of 100 members of the public and 30 members of staff who work at the centre.

While a small proportion of staff and public (10 per cent) felt that the opening of the pub would be a good idea, the majority of people surveyed felt that there would be problems with anti-social behaviour, littering and rowdiness.

Having taken into consideration all of the information provided, I wish to make the following recommendations:

The level of customer service that the centre currently provides is high and it is important that this is maintained. It is important to take into consideration the views and opinions of our customers and staff and to see things from their point of view. I believe that there would be a high risk involved if we were to allow the pub to serve alcoholic beverages from 11a.m. until 11p.m. and that problems with anti-social behaviour could develop. We have a responsibility to protect the public and to ensure that they are safe while in the centre.

(Continued)

(Continued)

> While it is important initially to obtain the views of the pub owners, I recommend that the pub is permitted to serve alcoholic beverages only from 11a.m. until 1p.m. and from 5p.m. until 7p.m. so as to reduce the risk of the above problems developing.

> I have recommended this course of action, as I believe it is in the best interests of the centre, its staff and more importantly our valued customers. This alternative course of action would be for a trial period only and providing there are no problems with anti-social behaviour, littering or rowdiness we could look to review the opening hours with a view to extending them. I am prepared to take full responsibility for monitoring the situation once the pub has been opened. I will keep you updated on progress.
>
> Customer Services Officer

The final step in creating your report is to use keywords and phrases when writing your response, which are relevant to the core competencies being assessed. The following are sentences and phrases that I used while creating my report that relate to a number of competency areas:

- 'The level of customer service that the centre currently provides is high and it is important that this is maintained' – relates to community and customer focus.

- 'It is important to take into consideration the views and opinions of our customers and staff and to see things from their point of view' – relates to respect for race and diversity.

- 'I believe that there would be a high risk involved if we were to allow the pub to serve alcoholic beverages from 11a.m. until 11p.m. and that problems with anti-social

behaviour could develop' – relates to problem solving and resilience.

- 'We have a responsibility to protect the public and to ensure that they are safe while in the centre' – relates to personal responsibility.

- 'While it is important initially to obtain the views of the pub owners, I recommend that the pub is permitted to serve alcoholic beverages only from 11a.m. until 1p.m. and from 5p.m. until 7p.m. so as to reduce the risk of the above problems developing' – relates to respect for race and diversity and also problem solving.

- 'I have recommended this course of action, as I believe it is in the best interests of the centre, its staff and more importantly our valued customers' – relates to customer focus.

- 'This alternative course of action would be for a trial period only and providing there are no problems with anti-social behaviour, littering or rowdiness we could look to review the opening hours with a view to extending them' – relates to problem solving and resilience.

- 'I am prepared to take full responsibility for monitoring the situation once the pub has been opened' – relates to personal responsibility.

- 'I will keep you updated on progress' – relates to team-working.

You will now see how important it is to learn the core competencies before you attend the assessment centre!

Before you have a go yourself at a number of report writing exercises I will provide you with some important hints and tips on how to create an effective report.

Important Tips to Help You Structure a Good Report

- Remember that you are being assessed against effective communication. This means creating a report that is concise, relevant and easy to read.

- Make sure you answer the question.

- Aim to make zero grammar, spelling or punctuation errors. If you are unsure about a word, do not use it.

- Create your report using a beginning, middle and an end as I have suggested.

- Use keywords and phrases from the core competencies. This is how the police will assess you.

- The amount that you write is down to you. Your focus should be on the quality of the report rather than quantity.

- Do not spend too much time reading the information and documentation provided. Spend a maximum of three minutes reading and digesting the documentation, and then spend at least 15 minutes writing your report. The final two minutes can be used for checking your report for errors.

Now that you know how to create a written report, try the sample exercises on the following pages. I have provided you with a template following each exercise for you to create your report. Don't forget to have a copy of the core competencies next to you when writing your practice reports. You will also need a copy of your Welcome Pack in order to respond to the questions effectively.

Sample written report exercises 2–6

Sample written report – exercise 2

You are the customer services officer for a fictitious retail centre. Your manager has asked you to compile a report regarding a number of complaints he has received from shop owners who state that rowdy youths are intimidating shop owners at the centre which is having a detrimental effect on their business generally and more importantly their takings. Visitor numbers at the centre are down 25 per cent over the last three months.

CCTV reports suggest that a gang of eight youths have been circling the centre during daylight shopping hours, often approaching customers and harassing them for spare change.

The local newspaper has become aware of these incidents and is sending a reporter along to interview your manager to see what the main problems are and what the centre intends to do about them.

Your report should detail your main findings and also your recommendations as to how the situation can be resolved.

Use the template on the following page to create your response.

Sample written report template

From:

To:

Subject:

Sample written report – exercise 3

You are the customer services officer for a fictitious retail centre. Your manager has received a request from the local authority Anti Truancy Group who wish to patrol the centre in groups of six people for a five-day period next month.

In their request the Anti Truancy Group has raised concerns that school children from the local area are congregating at the retail centre during school hours. CCTV cameras have confirmed these reports.

Local police have also confirmed in a recent report that anti-social behaviour in the area of the retail centre has increased by 15 per cent in the last four weeks alone.

You are to create a report for your manager that details your main findings and your recommendations.

Use the template on the following page to create your response.

Sample written report template

> **From:**
>
> **To:**
>
> **Subject:**

Sample written report – exercise 4

You are the customer services officer for a fictitious retail centre.

During a recent fire safety inspection at the retail centre, local fire officers found a large number of fire escapes to be blocked with cardboard boxes that had been stored by shop owners. They also noticed that many of the general areas were untidy and the housekeeping was below an acceptable standard. While the obstructions were removed at the time of the inspection, and the Fire Service will not be taking any further action, your manager is concerned that this type of incident will happen again.

He has asked you to create a report detailing your recommendations as to how this type of incident can be prevented in the future and also how the standard of housekeeping can be improved.

Use the template on the following page to create your response.

Sample written report template

From:

To:

Subject:

Sample written report – exercise 5

As the customer services officer for a fictitious retail centre you are required to provide your manager with a written report based on the following information.

Currently at the centre there are three unoccupied shops. A local charity would like to use one of the shops for a three-month period free of charge in order to raise money for charity by selling second-hand clothes and goods.

Your manager has already conducted a survey of all shop owners and staff at the centre to see what they feel about the proposal and the results are as follows:

- 15 per cent of shop owners support the idea.
- 5 per cent of shop owners do not have an opinion.
- 80 per cent of shop owners are against the idea.
- 90 per cent of staff at the centre support the idea.

You are to create a report detailing your main findings and recommendations based on the information provided.

Use the template on the following page to create your response.

Sample written report template

From:

To:

Subject:

Sample written report – exercise 6

You are the customer services officer for a fictitious retail centre.

Over the last four weeks the retail centre has been extremely busy and trade has been excellent. However, an issue has arisen whereby car owners are complaining that there are not enough car parking spaces at the centre. Many of the shop owners are complaining that they are losing trade as many potential customers are turning their backs on the centre during busy periods due to the lack of car parking spaces.

A petition has been signed by every shop owner at the centre supporting the removal of the disabled car parking spaces and reallocating them as standard car parking spaces in order to resolve the problem. There are currently 200 car parking spaces allocated at the centre specifically for disabled badge users.

Your manager is meeting with the shop owners in two days' time to discuss their proposal. He wants you to create a report detailing the main issues and your recommendations.

Use the template on the following page to create your response.

Sample written report template

From:

To:

Subject:

How to construct a letter

Now that you have had the opportunity to try out a number of written reports, we will take a look at how to create a letter or memo.

During the written exercise, you may be required to create a letter or memo in response to a complaint or other event while assuming the role of a customer services officer. Writing a letter, especially if it is in response to a complaint, can be quite a difficult task. However, with a little bit of preparation and practice you can improve your communication skills greatly.

Imagine that you are the manager of a retail centre or other similar complex. You receive a letter of complaint from a disgruntled member of the public. How do you respond? Obviously you need to be professional and impartial in your response, taking into account the customer's needs following their bad experience. Why do you need to do this? The answer is simple – you are providing a service to that particular customer and they feel you have let them down. Remember how important the core competencies are and what each one stands for!

Of course, it is important to investigate the complaint to ensure its validity but, in relation to dealing with complaints, you must try to resolve the issue carefully and effectively.

Take a look at the letter of complaint on the following page.

Sample letter of complaint

Mrs A. Nonymous
Fictitious Street
Fictown

Dear Sir/Madam,

I wish to make a complaint in relation to the service I received at your retail centre last week. I telephoned your main customer services desk to reserve a wheelchair as I was visiting the centre to carry out my weekly shop.

My English is not very good and I explained this to the receptionist, as she appeared to be getting impatient with me when I was trying to explain what I wanted. She began to raise her voice quite loud when I asked her to repeat what she had said. In the end she hung up on me due to her impatience. Naturally I feel extremely let down by the service I received that day and won't be using your centre anymore.

I believe that the receptionist should be told off for her poor handling of the issue and want to know what you are going to do about the matter.

I look forward to hearing from you very soon!

Yours faithfully,
Mrs A. Nonymous

Details of your investigation

After speaking to the receptionist, she admits to becoming impatient with the lady because her English was poor and it was a very busy day with lots of customers to serve. She says that the telephones kept ringing too and she'd not had a break for more than three hours.

So, you've gathered your information and confirmed that the complaint is a genuine one. How do you deal with it?

Preparing a written response to a letter

You have a number of choices when compiling your response. Do you think it is wise to explain that it was a busy period for the receptionist at that time and she had not had a break for a while? The answer should be no!

The problems at the retail centre in relation to the complaint are purely a management issue. There should be enough staff on the reception to deal with the majority of eventualities including telephone calls, bookings and taking payments, so it is not wise to make any excuses in your letter to the complainant.

When compiling your response you need to think of the core competencies and compose your letter in relation to them. In respect of this particular scenario, there is no excuse for the receptionist's behaviour and obviously there is a training issue that needs to be resolved. Your letter, therefore, should reflect the fact that you accept responsibility for the poor customer service the complainant has experienced. On the following page I have compiled a sample response.

Sample response to letter of complaint

Mr M Rogers
Customer Services Officer
The Retail Centre
Fictown

Dear Mrs Nonymous

I am writing in response to your letter of complaint following the service you received at this retail centre recently. Following an investigation into the complaint, which I personally conducted, I wish to apologise unreservedly for the poor level of customer service you received on that particular morning. It is the centre's policy that no customer shall receive less favourable treatment and I will be taking the relevant steps to ensure that this does not happen again.

The receptionist failed to provide you with the respect you deserved when dealing with your request to reserve a wheelchair for your forthcoming visit to the centre, and I fully appreciate how frustrating this must have been for you.

For your information I have formulated a plan to resolve this issue, including retraining to prevent a similar incident happening to any of our valued customers. With that in mind I want to thank you for bringing this problem to our attention, as without this kind of information we are unable to change or improve the service that we offer.

Once the problem has been resolved I will write to you again to inform you that the issue has been fully rectified. In the meantime, I have arranged for a dedicated wheelchair to made available to you at all times. All you need to do is arrive at the main customer services desk, provide your name, and the customer services assistant will assist you.

Please contact me on the above telephone number if you have any more comments, suggestions or questions. Once again, I apologise for your unfortunate experience.

Yours sincerely,

Customer Services Officer

After reading the sample response letter, do you think it is an appropriate response? The way to ascertain if your responses are correct is to match them against the core competencies relevant to that of a police officer.

Whatever the letter or response you have to compile during the assessment centre, you should always try to match the core competencies, just like you have been doing with the report writing exercises.

Everybody has different ways of learning but some of the most effective ways of learning the core competencies include:

- Writing down the core competencies every day for three weeks prior to your assessment day.

- Reading them at least once every day for three weeks prior to your assessment day.

- Carrying a small card around with you that has all of the core competencies written on it. Whenever you have a spare few minutes get out the card and read them.

- Ask someone to test you twice a week on the core competencies.

Now try the sample letter writing exercise on the following page.

Sample letter writing exercise

You are the customer services officer at a fictitious retail centre. Your manager has asked you to compile a report regarding a letter of complaint he has received from a customer, Mr Dobson. He has also requested that you compile a response to Mr Dobson's letter on his behalf.

This is a copy of Mr Dobson's letter to the manager.

---

15 Ficticious Road
Fictown

Dear Sir,

I am writing to you in order to complain about a situation that occurred at your retail centre recently. Last week I was visiting your centre with my granddaughter, when a gang of youths ran past us pushing me to the ground in the process. I am not very quick on my feet and I was struggling to get up so I decided to shout for assistance. I noticed a nearby security guard standing talking to customers so I waved to him for help. To my dismay he just waved back at me!

Luckily a kind young man came running to my aid and he helped me back onto my feet. As you can imagine my granddaughter was extremely upset about this and she does not want to return to the centre ever again.

I feel the fact that you allow gangs of youths to parade around the centre is disgusting. Even more appalling is the fact that the security guard failed to assist me in my time of need. I want to know what you are going to do about this and I eagerly await your reply.

Yours sincerely,

Mr J Dobson

Using the templates on the following pages you are required to:

1. Create a report recommending how this matter could be dealt with, addressed to your manager.

2. Write a letter to Mr J Dobson responding to his complaint.

You have 40 minutes in which to complete both responses.

Written report template

From:

To:

Subject:

Letter template

Customer Services Officer

The Retail Centre

Fictown

Important Tips for Passing the Written Exercises

- In the build-up to your assessment, practise plenty of report writing.

- Improve your spelling, grammar and punctuation.

- Do not use words that you find hard to spell.

- Make sure your handwriting is neat, tidy and legible.

- Use keywords and phrases from the core competencies.

- Construct your report in a concise manner using a beginning, middle and an end.

- Do not spend too long reading the documentation and paperwork that you are provided with. You need to allocate sufficient time to write your report or letter.

- Before you attend the assessment centre, make sure you are fully familiar with the role of the customer services manager and all other associated documentation. There is no excuse for not learning it prior to the day.

Golden Tip

When creating your written report or letter, use the documentation provided to make suggestions as to how the situation could be improved or addressed. I would also strongly recommend that you state the reasons why you have chosen that particular course of action. Where appropriate, deal with the issue in a constructive manner and always use correct spelling and grammar.

CHAPTER 9
THE ROLE-PLAY/ INTERACTIVE EXERCISES

At the police officer assessment centre you will have to deal with four interactive exercises or role plays as they are otherwise called. The type of situation that you will be confronted with varies greatly. However, examples of the types of exercises that have been used in the past include the following:

- A manager of a store that is inside a fictitious retail centre wants to discuss an issue with you that relates to the lack of security.

- A customer who has been shopping at a fictitious retail centre wants to talk to you about a conversation they have had with another customer.

- A school teacher who has been visiting a fictitious retail centre would like to discuss an issue with you regarding his/her pupils.

- A member of staff who works at a fictitious retail centre would like to discuss an issue with you.

The situation that you will have to deal with is irrelevant. It is how you interact with the role-play actor and what you say that is important. You must be able to demonstrate the police officer core competencies during each role-play scenario. Examples of how you would achieve this include:

- Dealing with the role-play actor in a sensitive and supportive manner.

- Having respect for people's views and feelings.

- Seeing issues from others' points of view.

- Ask relevant questions to clarify the situation.

- Listening to people's needs and interests.

- Respecting confidentiality where appropriate.

- Presenting an appropriate image.

- Trying to sort out customers' problems as soon as possible.

- Make reference to any supporting documentation, policies or procedures.

- Confirming that the customer is happy with your offered solution.

- Keeping customers updated on any progress that you make.

It is crucial that you learn the core competencies and are also able to demonstrate them during each exercise.

This part of the selection process will be split into two five-minute parts. The first part will consist of the preparation phase and the second part will be the actual activity phase for which you'll be assessed. I will now explain each phase in detail.

The preparation phase

During the five-minute preparation phase you will be provided with the actual scenario, either on a card or sheet of paper. You may also be provided with additional documentation that is relevant to the scenario that you'll be required to deal with. You will be taken to a desk or a separate room where you will have just five minutes in which to prepare for the activity phase. During the preparation phase you will be allowed to take notes and then use them during the activity phase. At the end of the activity phase you will normally be required to hand in your notes to the assessor. You will not be permitted to take any writing utensils into the activity phase.

Having been through this type of role-play assessment, I found that learning the Welcome Pack prior to the assessment day made my life a lot easier. The preparation phase was easy, simply because I knew my role as customer services officer inside out. I knew the code of conduct, the equality policy statement, and all other relevant information that was applicable to my role. As soon as I read the role-play scenario I knew exactly what I was required to do. Although the preparation phase is not assessable, you must still use the time wisely. This is how I recommend you use the time:

- Quickly read the scenario and any supporting information/ documentation. If you have already studied the Welcome Pack prior to assessment your life will be a lot easier.

- Once you have studied the scenario and any additional information/documentation you should then separate relevant information from irrelevant information, just like you did during the written report writing stage. Write down brief notes as to what you think is relevant.

- You now need to cross match any relevant information from the scenario with procedures, policies and your responsibilities that are provided in the Welcome Pack. For

example, if within the scenario it becomes apparent that somebody from the centre is being bullied or harassed, you will need to know, use and make reference to the equality policy statement during the activity phase of the assessment. Another example would be where a child has been reported missing. If this was the case then you would possibly wish to make use of the security guards, the tannoy system and also the CCTV cameras that are based around the centre.

- I would now recommend that you write down a step-by-step approach of what you intend to do during the activity stage. An example of this may be as follows:

Step 1
Introduce myself to the role actor and ask him/her how I can help.

(Remember to be polite and respectful and treat the role-play actor in a sensitive and supportive manner. You are being assessed against the core competency of respect for race and diversity during every role-play scenario.)

Step 2
Listen to them carefully and ask relevant questions to establish the facts.

(How, When, Where, Why, Who)

Step 3
Clarify the information received to check I have understood exactly what has happened.

Step 4

Provide a suitable solution to the problem or situation and tell the role-play actor what I intend to do.

(Remember to use keywords and phrases from the core competencies.)

Step 5

Check to confirm that the role-play actor is happy with my solution.

Provide a final summary of what I intend to do and ask them if there is anything else I can help them with.

(Tell the role-play actor that you will take personal responsibility for solving the problem and that you will keep them updated on progress.)

Once you have made your notes and created a plan of action you are now ready to go through to the activity phase. Before we move on to this stage of the role-play assessment I will provide you with a further explanation of how you may wish to approach the preparation phase using a sample scenario.

Sample role-play exercise 1

You are the customer services manager at a fictitious retail centre. A member of your staff approaches you and tells you that she has been bullied by another member of staff. The woman is clearly upset by the situation and she wants you to take action.

How to prepare

If you have already taken the time to study the Welcome Pack prior to attending the assessment then the first thing that will spring to your mind will be the equality policy statement. Within the statement you will find specific details about how

to deal with situations of this nature and it is essential that you follow each step carefully. Remember that one of the assessable core competencies requires you to follow and refer to policies and procedures.

Using my five-step plan, the following is how I might deal with this type of situation:

Step 1 – I would walk into the activity room and introduce myself to the role-play actor. I would ask them sensitively what the problem was and how I could help them. If there was a chair available in the room then I would ask them to sit down.

Step 2 – I would listen very carefully to what they had to say and sympathise where appropriate. I would then start to establish the facts of the case asking them relevant questions such as:

- How long had the bullying been going on for?

- Who was involved and what had they been doing/saying?

- Were any other people involved?

- Have there been any witnesses to this incident?

- Had they asked the other person to stop bullying them and if so what was their reaction?

Step 3 – I would then clarify and confirm with the role-play actor that I had gathered the correct facts.

Step 4 – At this stage I would take full control of the situation and tell the role-play actor what I intended to do about the situation. I would make reference at this stage to the equality policy statement and I would use it as a basis for solving the problem. I would also use keywords and phrases that matched the core competencies.

Step 5 – During the final stages of the role-play activity I would check to confirm that the role-play actor was happy with my

solution. I would provide them with a final summary of what I intended to do and I would ask them if there was anything else that I could help them with. I would also confirm at this stage that I would take personal responsibility for resolving the problem and that I would keep them updated on progress as and when it occurred.

Once the five-minute preparation phase is complete a buzzer will sound and you will then move on to the activity phase of the assessment.

The activity phase

The activity phase will again last for five minutes and it is during this phase that you are required to interact with the role-play actor.

During the activity phase there will be an assessor in the room whose responsibility it is to assess you against the core competencies. Try to ignore them and concentrate fully on how you interact with the role-play actor. There may also be a third person in the room who will be there to shadow the assessor or for quality assurance purposes. During the activity phase you will be assessed on what you did and how you did it. You will usually be graded from A to D with the highest score earning you an A to the weakest score earning you a D.

Obviously, you want to aim for an A but don't be disheartened if you feel that you haven't done well on a particular exercise, as you can make up your grades in another. However, if you score a D against the core competency of respect for race and diversity then you will fail the entire assessment.

During the previous sample role-play exercise (exercise 1) we focused on a complaint made by a member of staff who claimed that she was being bullied by another member of staff. Within the equality policy statement you will find suggested courses of action. The options here may suggest that the person asks the offender to stop, the problem is discussed

with an appropriate person (you) or the option is available to make a formal complaint.

Below I have provided you with some suggested responses to this type of exercise followed by an explanation. Most of these can be applied to similar exercises surrounding harassment cases, although you should judge every situation separately and act according to the brief.

Sample responses and actions to exercise 1

Response
Thank you for coming to see me today. I understand that you have a problem with another member of staff?

Explanation
During this type of response you are demonstrating a level of customer care and you are focusing on the needs of the individual. Remember to use open body language and never become confrontational, defensive or aggressive.

Response
Would you be able to tell me exactly what has happened and how this has affected you? I will also need to ask you who's been bullying you, where it has been occurring and on how many occasions including dates and times.

Explanation
Again you are focusing on the needs of the individual, which is important. Try to look and sound genuine and also use suitable facial expressions. In order to 'problem solve' you must first ask questions and gather the facts of the incident.

Response
It must be very difficult for you to bring this matter to my attention; you are to be praised for this course of action.

Explanation
During this response you are demonstrating a caring nature and you are providing a high level of service.

Response

Have you asked him to stop or have you informed anybody else of this situation?

and

Are you aware of this happening to anybody else?

Explanation

Here you are gathering the facts, which will help you provide a suitable resolution to the problem.

Response

The company equality policy in relation to this kind of alleged behaviour is quite clear, it states XYZ. It will NOT be tolerated and I can assure you the matter will be dealt with.

Explanation

During this response you are detailing the company equality policy. This demonstrates to the assessor that you are fully aware of the policies and procedures – this will gain you higher scores. You are also stating that this type of behaviour is not accepted and you are, therefore, challenging the inappropriate behaviour in line with the police officer core competencies.

Response

Before I detail my solution to this problem I want to first of all confirm the details of the case. Please can you confirm that . . .

Explanation

During this response I am confirming and checking that the details I have obtained are correct.

Response

Please be aware that you can make a formal complaint if you so wish. Your feelings and wishes are paramount during my investigation. What would you like to happen from here? Would you like to make a formal complaint against the individual concerned?

Explanation

By asking the complainant what they want to do, you are demonstrating that you are putting their needs first and you are respecting confidentiality.

Response

Let me assure you that this matter will be dealt with as a priority but in the meantime I will place another member of staff with you so that you can work in a comfortable environment. Are you happy with this course of action?

Explanation

Here you are taking action to resolve the problem. You are also informing the person how you intend to resolve it. Finally you are checking that the person is happy with your actions.

Response

May I thank you again for bringing this matter to my attention; I will keep you fully informed of all progress. I wish to inform you that I will be taking personal responsibility for resolving this issue. Is there anything else I can do for you?

Explanation

Finally you are demonstrating a high level of customer service and also checking if there is anything else that you can do for the person. You are also taking personal responsibility for resolving the issue. It is important to tell the person that you will keep them informed of the outcome of any investigation.

Top Tips for Preparing for the Role-play Exercises

- Learn the core competencies that are being assessed and be able to 'act' out each one.

- A good way to practise for these exercises is to ask a friend or family relative to 'role-play' the sample exercises contained within this book.

- When practising the exercises, try to pick someone you know who will make it difficult for you. Also, try to resolve

---

each issue in a calm but effective manner, in line with the core competencies.

- You may wish to purchase a copy of the *How to pass the Police Officer Role Play* DVD, now available at www. how2become.co.uk.

Top Tips for Passing the Role-play Exercises

- Use the preparation time wisely.

- Learn the pre-assessment material before you go to the assessment. This will make your life much easier.

- Remain calm during every role play. Even if the actor becomes confrontational, it is essential that you remain calm.

- If at any time during the role-play activity phase the role-play actor uses language that is either inappropriate (including swearing), discriminatory or uses any form of harassment then you must challenge it immediately. When challenging this kind of behaviour you must do so in an assertive manner without becoming aggressive. Always be polite and respectful at all times.

- Use effective listening skills during the role-play exercises and ask questions in order to gather the facts.

- Once you have gathered the facts of the case or situation then solve the problem.

On the following pages I have provided you with a number of sample role-play exercises. To begin with, read each exercise carefully and then make notes in the box provided, detailing how you might deal with the situation. Make sure you have a copy of the core competencies to hand when making your notes.

Next, ask a friend or relative to act out each scenario so you can practise dealing with it.

Sample role-play exercise 2

You are the customer services officer at a fictitious retail centre. A school teacher has lost a pupil in the shopping centre and he wants to discuss the matter with you. He is very annoyed that it took him so long to find your office. He states that there were no security staff around and his pupil has now been missing for 15 minutes. He wants to know what you intend to do about it.

How to prepare and possible actions

- To begin with, you should study the 'OPERATIONS' information about the centre. What does it say that possibly relates to the above scenario? Is there any CCTV?

- Could the security staff help look for missing persons?

- Is there a police station within the complex and can the police be used to respond to situations like this?

- Request the attendance of the police immediately.

- Keep the teacher in the office with you to provide further information to the police about the missing child.

- Gather information about the missing child – How old are they? What are they wearing? What is their name? Are there any distinguishing features? Where were they last seen?

- Try to reassure the teacher that everything will be all right.

- If the shopping centre has a loudspeaker system, use it to transmit a 'missing persons' message.

- Consider positioning a member of the security team at each exit to prevent anybody walking out with the child.

On the next page I have provided a sample response to this exercise. Read it before using the box on the following page to make notes on how you would deal with this situation.

Sample responses and actions to exercise 2

Hello Sir, my name is Richard and I'm the customer services manager for this centre. I understand that one of your pupils has gone missing in the centre – is that correct? (Establish exactly what has happened.)

Firstly, can I reassure you that the police have been called and they are on their way. I have also put a security guard at each exit to look out for the missing child. In the meantime I would like to take some details from you. Please can you give me a full description of the missing pupil, including their name? (Make a note of the description.)

How long have they been missing and where were they last seen?

Have you or anybody else been looking for the missing person and have you reported this to anybody else yet?

Is there a possibility that they might have wandered off to their favourite shop or gone somewhere else with another parent who was in the group?

Do you think they would understand their own name if we broadcast this over the loudspeaker system?

OK Sir, thank you for providing me with these details. This is what I propose to do. First, I will check the CCTV cameras to see if we can locate the missing child. I will also brief all members of staff at the centre, including the security guards, with the missing child's description. I will also put out a tannoy announcement asking the missing child to go to the nearest customer services desk where a member of staff will meet them.

In addition, I will put the registered nurse on standby so that she can treat the child for shock if appropriate. In the meantime, please stay here until the police arrive, as it is important you provide them with more information. Let me reassure you that we will do everything we possibly can to locate the missing person. I am taking personal responsibility for resolving this issue and will keep you updated on progress.

Notes for sample role-play exercise 2

Sample role-play exercise 3

You are the customer services officer at a fictitious retail centre. One of the centre store managers wants to see you about a gang of youths who are standing outside his shop behaving in an anti-social manner, swearing and obstructing customers from entering his shop. He is very annoyed at the situation and is losing money because potential customers are not allowed to shop in comfort without feeling threatened.

How to prepare and possible actions

- To begin with you should study the 'OPERATIONS' information and the 'CODE OF CONDUCT' information in the Welcome Pack. What do they say that possibly relates to the above scenario? Is this kind of behaviour tolerated? Can people who behave in such a manner be escorted from the centre and should the police be involved? Can you involve the security staff or use the CCTV cameras to provide the police with evidence?

- Remember that the manager is annoyed at the situation and therefore you may have to defuse a confrontational situation in the first instance. Remember to be firm but stay calm and never become confrontational yourself.

On the next page I have provided a sample response to this exercise. Read it before using the box on the following page to make notes on how you would deal with this situation.

Sample responses and actions to exercise 3

Hello Sir, thank you for coming to see me today. My name is Richard and I am the customer services officer at the centre. I understand there is an issue with a gang of youths outside your shop? (Establish the facts of the incident by asking relevant questions.)

Can I, first of all, say that I fully understand how frustrating this must be for you as you are losing customers all the time the problem is present. I wish to apologise unreservedly for any problems that you are experiencing at the centre. I have called the police and they are on their way. In the meantime, it is important that I take into consideration your feelings and opinions. Therefore, please can you provide me with some information about what has been happening? (Make a note of what has happened.)

How many people are there outside your shop? Has this happened before or is this the first time?

Have you reported it to anyone else? Can you provide me with a description of the people who are creating the problem? What type of language are they using?

May I reassure you, Sir, that in line with the code of conduct, the centre will not tolerate any form of anti-social behaviour and we have the power to remove people from the building and prevent them from re-entering at a later time. While we await the arrival of the police I will try to see if the CCTV cameras have picked up anything.

I am sorry that you have had to go through this experience, Sir, but we will do everything we can to rectify the problem. As the customer services officer for the centre it is my responsibility to ensure you receive the highest standard of customer care. With that in mind, I will be taking full responsibility for resolving this issue and I will keep you updated of all progress as and when it occurs. Is there anything else I can help you with?

Notes for sample role-play exercise 3

Sample role-play exercise 4

You are the customer services officer at a fictitious retail centre. A customer would like to see you about an issue surrounding a dog that is in the shopping centre. She is very annoyed that a dog has been allowed to enter the shopping centre and wants to know what you are going to do about it. The dog is an 'assistance dog' for a visually impaired customer.

How to prepare and possible actions

- To begin with, you should study the 'OPERATIONS' information, the 'CODE OF CONDUCT' information and the 'EQUALITY POLICY' statement relating to the centre. What do they say that possibly relates to the above scenario? Are 'assistance dogs' permitted? If the answer is 'yes' then the person may not have any grounds for complaint. However, it is important to listen to the complaint before responding in a calm but firm manner.

- Remember to be confident in your handling of the situation and refer to the policy of the centre for such issues. Do not get drawn into personal opinions but stick to the code of conduct for the centre and apply it accordingly.

On the next page I have provided a sample response to this exercise. Read it before using the box on the following page to make notes on how you would deal with this situation.

Sample responses and actions to exercise 4

Hello Madam, my name is Richard and I am the customer services officer for the centre. Thank you for coming to see me today. I understand there is an issue with a dog in the shopping centre. Please would you explain what the problem is?

Listen to the customer's complaint and choose an appropriate moment to respond. If at any time the customer uses inappropriate or discriminatory language then you must challenge it in an appropriate manner. It is important that you ask relevant questions in order to establish the facts of the case.

While dogs are not permitted in the shopping centre, there is an exception for 'assistance dogs' like the one you have just described. Our code of conduct states that assistance dogs for the visually impaired are permitted in the centre. The centre will not discriminate against persons with disabilities and we will do everything we can to help their shopping experience to be a pleasurable one.

We have a legal requirement to allow 'assistance dogs' into the centre and if we were to ignore these rules we would be in contravention of the law. I am sorry, Madam, but in this instance I am unable to take any action. Thank you for coming to see me and have a good day.

Notes for sample role-play exercise 4

Top Tips and Guidance

- Please note that the sample scenarios provided within this book are examples only and they will not be the scenarios that you are assessed against at the assessment centre. While some of them may be similar, you must treat each case based on the information provided and the facts surrounding the scenario. It is not the scenario that is important but how you deal with it.

- Remember never to get annoyed or show signs of anger during the interactive exercises.

- The members of staff who are carrying out the fictitious roles may try to make the situation difficult to deal with. They may come across in a confrontational manner during the role-play scenarios so be prepared for this. Don't let it put you on the back foot and remember that they are trying to test your ability to defuse confrontational situations. You must remain in control at all times and treat the role-play actor in a sensitive and supportive manner.

- Most importantly, make sure you remember to respect equality and diversity at all times. You will be assessed in this area during every scenario.

- Challenge any inappropriate behaviour immediately during the role-play scenarios. Be firm where appropriate but do not become confrontational.

- Use keywords and phrases from the core competencies where possible.

- Finally, remember to be confident and firm whenever required. However, do respect your role as a customer services manager and provide a high level of service.

Golden Tips

- Always try to deal with the role-play actor in a sensitive and supportive manner.

- During the role-play activity phase ask appropriate questions in order to gather information surrounding the case.

- Once you have gathered your information you must clarify.

- Explain any relevant documentation in your responses. This will gain you higher marks.

- Make sensible suggestions about how you think you can improve the situation.

- Always interact with the role-play actor in a clear and constructive manner.

- Be sure to deal with the issues directly in accordance with the Welcome Pack and any other documentation provided.

THE POLICE OFFICER INTERVIEW

CHAPTER 10
THE ASSESSMENT CENTRE INTERVIEW

As part of the police officer assessment you will normally be required to sit an interview that is based around the core competencies. Under normal circumstances the interview board will consist of two or three people. These can be from either the uniformed side of the service or support staff.

It is important to remember that while you will be nervous you should try not to let this get in the way of your success. Police officers, in general, are confident people who have the ability to rise to a challenge and perform under difficult and pressurised situations. Treat the interview no differently from this. You ARE capable of becoming a police officer and the nerves that you have on the day are only natural, in fact they will help you to perform better if you have prepared sufficiently. The crucial element to your success, as with the rest of the selection process, is your preparation.

The police interview board will have a number of set questions to choose from and, while these are constantly changing, they will usually form part of the police officer core competencies.

Before attending your interview ensure that you read, digest and understand the police core competencies. Without these it will be difficult to pass the interview.

The interview will last for approximately 20 to 30 minutes depending on the length of your responses. During this time you will be asked a number of questions about specific situations and experiences that are important to the role of the police officer.

These questions will be based around the police officer core competencies and you will be provided with details of these in your Welcome Pack, which the police will send you prior to your assessment. The core competencies that are usually assessed are as follows:

- Respect for race and diversity
- Teamworking
- Problem solving
- Resilience
- Effective communication (not assessed through direct questioning)

You will be allowed up to five minutes to answer each question so don't be afraid to use the time you have. You may find during the interview that the interviewer asks you probing questions. Probing questions are designed to help you in giving your response so listen to what he or she has to say.

Preparing for the assessment centre interview

When preparing for the assessment centre competency based interview you should try to formulate responses to questions that surround the assessable core competencies. The responses that you provide should be specific examples of where you have experienced that particular scenario. In your Welcome Pack, which will be sent to you approximately

two weeks before the date of your assessment, you should find examples of the core competencies relevant to a police officer. These are the criteria that you will be scored against so it is worthwhile reading them beforehand and trying to structure your answers around them as best you can. For example, one of the sections you will be assessed against could be 'Respect for Race and Diversity'. You may be asked a question where you have to give an example of where you have had to respect other people's opinions and views that are from a different culture or background than your own. Try to think of an example where you have had to do this and structure your answer around the core competencies required, for example you are respectful to people and treat them with dignity while taking into consideration their views and opinions. Show that you are sensitive to language and use it in an appropriate manner.

On the following pages I have provided you with an example of how your response could be structured if you were responding to a question that was based around the core competency of personal responsibility. While this core competency will not normally be assessed during the interview, the sample response provided will give you a good indication of how you may wish to structure your responses.

Remember that the following sample question and response is for example purposes only.

Sample interview question based around the core competency of personal responsibility

Please provide an example of where you have taken personal responsibility to arrange or organise an event or situation.

After reading an appeal in my local paper from a local charity, I decided to try to raise money for this worthwhile cause by organising a charity car wash day at the local school during the summer holidays. I decided that the event would take place in a month's time, which would give me enough time to organise it.

I set about organising the event and soon realised that I had made a mistake in trying to do everything on my own, so I arranged for two of my work colleagues to assist me. Once they had agreed to help I asked one of them to organise the booking of the school and arrange sponsorship in the form of buckets, sponges and car wash soap to use on the day, so that we did not have to use our own money to buy them. I asked the second person to arrange advertising in the local newspaper and radio stations so that we could let the local community know about our charity car wash event, which would, in turn, hopefully bring in more money on the day for the charity.

Following a successful advertising campaign, I was inundated with calls from local newspapers about our event and it was becoming hard work having to keep talking to them and explaining what the event was all about. But I knew that this information was important if we were to raise our target of £500.

Everything was going well right up to the morning of the event, when I realised we had not got the key to open the school gates. It was the summer holidays so the caretaker was not there to open the gates for us.

Not wanting to let everyone down, I jumped in my car and made my way down to the caretaker's house. I managed to wake him up and get the key just in time before the car wash

event was due to start. In the end the day was a great success and we all managed to raise £600 for the charity.

Now that we have taken a look at a sample response, let's explore how the response matched the core competency.

How the response matches the core competency being assessed

In order to demonstrate how effective the above response is, we have broken it down into individual responses and provided the core competency area that it matches.

Response
. . . I decided to try to raise money for this worthwhile cause by organising a charity car wash day . . .

Core competency matched
- Takes on tasks without being asked
- Uses initiative

Response
. . . which would give me enough time to organise it.

Core competency matched
- Is conscientious in completing work on time

Response
I set about organising the event and soon realised that I had made a mistake in trying to do everything on my own, so I arranged for two of my work colleagues to assist me.

Core competency matched
- Takes responsibility for problems and tasks
- Takes personal responsibility for own actions

- Uses initiative
- Is open, honest and genuine

Response
. . . arrange sponsorship in the form of buckets, sponges and car wash soap to use on the day, so that we did not have to use our own money to buy them.

Core competency matched
- Uses initiative

Response
Following a successful advertising campaign, I was inundated with calls from local newspapers about our event and it was becoming hard work having to keep talking to them and explaining what the event was all about. But I knew that this information was important if we were to raise our target of £500.

Core competency matched
- Focuses on a task even if it is routine
- Uses initiative

Response
Not wanting to let everyone down, I jumped in my car and made my way down to the caretaker's house. I managed to wake him up and get the key just in time before the car wash event was due to start.

Core competency matched
- Follows things through to a satisfactory conclusion
- Uses initiative
- Takes personal responsibility for own actions
- Keeps promises and does not let colleagues down
- Takes responsibility for problems and tasks

The explanations above have, I hope, highlighted the importance of matching the core competencies that are being assessed.

When you receive your Welcome Pack, make sure you read it thoroughly and prepare yourself fully for the interview. Preparation is everything and by reading exactly what is required you will increase your chances of success on the day.

On the following pages I have provided you with a number of sample assessment centre interview questions that are based around the core competencies. Following each question I have provided some useful tips and advice on how you may consider answering the question.

Once you have read the question and the tips, use the template to create a response using your own experiences and knowledge.

Sample competency based interview questions 1–6

Sample competency based interview question I

Please provide an example of where you have worked as part of a team to achieve a difficult task.

Tips for Constructing Your Response

- Think of a situation where you volunteered to work with a team in order to achieve a difficult task. It is better to say that you volunteered, as opposed to being asked to get involved by another person.

- Those candidates who can provide an example of where they achieved the task despite the constraints of time will generally score better.

- Consider structuring your response in the following manner:

    Step 1
    Explain what the situation was and how you became involved.

    Step 2
    Explain who else was involved and what the task was.

    Step 3
    Explain why the task was difficult and whether there were any time constraints.

    Step 4
    Explain how it was decided who would carry out what task.

    Step 5
    Explain what had to be done and how you overcame any obstacles or hurdles.

Step 6

Explain what the result/outcome was. Try to make the
result positive as a result of your actions.

Now use the template on the following page to construct
your own response to this question, based on your own
experiences and knowledge.

Sample competency based interview question 1

> **Please provide an example of where you have worked as part of a team to achieve a difficult task.**

Examples of probing questions

1. Would you have done anything different next time?

2. How did the end result make you feel?

Sample competency based interview question 2

Provide an example of where you have challenged someone's behaviour that was either discriminatory or inappropriate. What did you do and what did you say?

Top Tips for Constructing Your Response

- Read carefully the core competency that relates to respect for race and diversity before constructing your response.

- When challenging this type of behaviour, make sure you remain calm at all times and never become aggressive or confrontational.

- Consider structuring your response in the following manner:

  Step 1 – Explain what the situation was and how you became involved.

  Step 2 – Explain who else was involved and why you felt that the behaviour was inappropriate or discriminatory. What was it that was being said or done?

  Step 3 – Explain what you said or did and why.

  Step 4 – Explain how the other person/people reacted when you challenged the behaviour.

  Step 5 – Explain what the end result was. Try to make the result positive following your actions.

  Step 6 – Finally, explain why you think it was that the people/person behaved as they did.

Now use the template on the following page to construct your own response to this question, based on your own experiences and knowledge.

Sample competency based interview question 2

Provide an example of where you have challenged someone's behaviour that was either discriminatory or inappropriate. What did you do and what did you say?

Examples of probing questions

1. How did you feel when you were challenging their behaviour?

2. How did the person or people react when you challenged their behaviour?

Sample competency based interview question 3

Provide an example of where you have helped somebody from a culture or background different from your own. What did you do and what did you say?

Top Tips for Constructing Your Response

- Read carefully the core competency that relates to respect for race and diversity before constructing your response.

- Think of a situation where you have gone out of your way to help somebody.

- Try to use keywords and phrases from the core competency in your response.

- Consider structuring your response in the following manner:

Step 1
Explain what the situation was and how you became involved. It is better to say that you volunteered to be involved, rather than to say that you were asked to.

Step 2
Explain who else was involved and why they needed your help or assistance?

Step 3
Explain what you said or did and why. Also explain any factors you took into consideration when helping them.

Step 4
Explain how the other person/people reacted to your help or assistance. Did they benefit from it?

Step 5
Explain what the end result was. Try to make the result positive following your actions.

Now use the template on the following page to construct your own response to this question, based on your own experiences and knowledge.

Sample competency based interview question 3

> **Provide an example of where you have helped somebody from a culture or background different from your own. What did you do and what did you say?**

Examples of probing questions

1. What did you learn from this experience?
2. Would you have done anything differently?

Sample competency based interview question 4

Provide an example of where you have solved a difficult problem. What did you do?

Top Tips for Constructing Your Response

- Read carefully the core competency that relates to problem solving.

- Try to include keywords and phrases from the core competency in your response to this question.

- Consider structuring your response in the following manner:

Step 1
Explain what the situation was and why you were under pressure.

Step 2
Explain what steps you took in order to complete the task on time.

Step 3
Explain why you took that particular action, and also the thought process behind your actions.

Step 4
Explain the barriers or difficulties that you had to overcome in order to finish the task on time.

Step 5
Explain what the end result was. Try to make the result positive following your actions.

Now use the template on the following page to construct your own response to this question, based on your own experiences and knowledge.

Sample competency based interview question 4

> **Provide an example of where you have solved a difficult problem. What did you do?**

Examples of probing questions

1. What did you learn from this experience?

2. Could you have done it any better?

Sample competency based interview question 5

Provide an example of where you have completed a task despite pressure from others. What did you do and what did you say?

Top Tips for Constructing Your Response

- Read carefully the core competency that relates to problem solving.

- Try to include keywords and phrases from the core competency in your response to this question.

- Consider structuring your response in the following manner:

Step 1
Explain what the situation was and why the problem was difficult.

Step 2
Explain what action you took in order to solve the difficult problem.

Step 3
Explain why you took that particular action, and also the thought process behind your actions.

Step 4
Explain the barriers or difficulties that you had to overcome.

Step 5
Explain what the end result was. Try to make the result positive following your actions.

Now use the template on the following page to construct your own response to this question, based on your own experiences and knowledge.

Sample competency based interview question 5

Provide an example of where you have completed a task despite pressure from others. What did you do and what did you say?

Examples of probing questions

1. What did you learn from this experience and would you do anything differently next time?

2. What did the other people think about what you did? Were they happy with your work?

Sample competency based interview question 6

Please provide an example of where you have had to make a difficult decision, despite pressure from other people.

Top Tips for Constructing Your Response

- Read carefully the core competency that relates to resilience.

- Try to include keywords and phrases from the core competency in your response to this question.

- Consider structuring your response in the following manner:

Step 1

Explain what the situation was and who was involved.

Step 2

Explain why the decision was difficult and what pressure you were under.

Step 3

Explain what you did and why you did it.

Step 4

Explain what the other people did or said in reaction to your decision, and explain why you think they reacted as they did.

Step 5

Explain what the end result was. Try to provide a positive outcome to the situation.

Now use the template on the following page to construct your own response to this question, based on your own experiences and knowledge.

Sample competency based interview question 6

Please provide an example of where you have had to make a difficult decision, despite pressure from other people.

Examples of probing questions

1. What did you learn from this experience and would you do anything differently next time?

2. Why do you think the other people reacted as they did?

How to improve your scores through effective communication

While you will not normally be questioned directly in relation to oral communication during the interview, you will be assessed indirectly.

During the assessment centre competency based interview, the panel will be looking to see how you communicate and also how you structure your responses to the interview questions.

Consider the following points, both during the interview and while responding to the interview questions:

- When you walk into the interview room stand up straight and introduce yourself. Be polite and courteous at all times and try to come across in a pleasant manner. The panel will be assessing you as soon as you walk through the door so make sure you make a positive first impression.

- Do not sit down in the interview chair until you are invited to do so. This is good manners.

- When you sit down in the interview chair, sit up straight and do not fidget or slouch. It is acceptable to use hand gestures when explaining your responses to the questions, but don't over do it as they can become a distraction.

- Structure your responses to the questions in a logical manner – this is very important. When responding to an interview question, start at the beginning and work your way through in a concise manner, and at a pace that is easy for the panel to listen to.

- Speak clearly and in a tone that is easy for the panel to hear. Be confident in your responses.

- When talking to the panel use eye contact but be careful not to look at them in an intimidating manner.

- Consider wearing some form of formal outfit to the interview, such as a suit. While you will not be assessed on the type of outfit you wear to the interview, it will make you come across in a more professional manner.

Top Golden Interview Tips

- Always provide 'specific' examples to the questions being asked.

- During your responses try to outline your contributions and also provide evidence of the competency area that is being assessed.

- Speak clearly, use correct English and structure your responses in a logical and concise manner.

CHAPTER II
THE FINAL INTERVIEW

Some police forces have started to introduce what is called a final interview. The final interview is in addition to the assessment centre competency based interview and will take on a different format.

Within this section of the guide I have provided some insider tips and advice on how to prepare for the interview, the type of questions that you may be asked, and also how to respond to them.

To begin with, let's take a look at a few more details relating to the final interview.

About the interview

The interview will usually take place at the force's training centre or a similar establishment. The purpose of the final interview is to allow the force to ask you questions that are outside of the competencies that have been assessed at the assessment centre. In essence, it allows the force to find out more about you, your application, your motivations for wanting to become a police officer, and what you know about

the role and the force that you are applying to join. They may also ask you questions that are based around what you might do in a given situation.

The interview panel will normally consist of two to three people and is usually made up of uniformed police officers and also a member of the human resources team. The length of the interview will very much depend on the questions the panel wants to ask you and also how long your responses are. In general terms, the interview will normally last for approximately one hour.

How to prepare for the final interview

If you have made it this far in the selection process then you have done tremendously well. The Police Force is certainly interested in recruiting you but it wants to find out more about you first. There are a number of areas that you will need to prepare for and these are as follows:

- Interview technique

- The reasons why you want to become a police officer and what you know about the role

- Application form

- What you know about the force you are applying to join

- Situational interview questions.

Now that we understand how to prepare for the interview, let us break down each particular section in detail.

Interview technique

Many candidates spend little or no time improving or developing their interview technique. It is important that you spend sufficient time on this area, as it will allow your confidence to improve.

The way to improve interview technique is to carry out what we call a mock interview. Mock interviews are where you ask a friend or relative to ask you a number of interview questions under formalised interview conditions. This can be achieved at home across your dining-room table or even while sitting on the chairs in your living room.

During the mock interview you should work on your interview technique. The mock interview will also give you a valuable opportunity to try out your responses to a number of sample interview questions that are contained within this guide. It is important that your mock interviewer provides you with constructive feedback. Do not choose somebody who will tell you that you were great, even when you weren't, as this just defeats the whole purpose of a mock interview.

To carrying out a mock interview:

- Choose a quiet room in the house or at another suitable location.

- Set the room up with a table and two chairs.

- The interviewer then invites you into the room and the interview commences. Don't forget to be polite and courteous to the interviewer and only sit down when invited to do so.

- When the interviewer asks you the questions, respond to them in a logical manner and in a tone of voice that can be heard easily.

- Throughout the mock interview, work hard on your technique and style. Sit upright at all times and look at the interviewer using soft eye contact. Do not fidget or slouch in the interview chair.

- Once the interview is over, ask the interviewer for feedback on your performance.

- Repeat the process at least three times until you are comfortable with your technique and style of answering.

The reasons why you want to become a police officer and what you know about the role

During the final interview the panel may ask you questions that relate to why you want to become a police officer and, in particular, what you know about the role.

Why do you want to become a police officer?

In the build-up to your interview you need to think carefully about why you want to become a police officer and what it is exactly that has attracted you to the role. Those candidates who want to become a police officer so that they can 'catch criminals' and 'ride about in a police car with the blue lights flashing' will score poorly. Only you will know the exact reasons why you want to join the police, but here are some examples of good reasons and examples of poor reasons.

Good reasons to give:

- To make a difference to your community, make it a safer place and reduce any fear that the public may have.

- To carry out a job that is worthwhile and one that makes a difference.

- The variety of the job and the different challenges that you will face on a day-to-day basis.

- The chance to work with a highly professional team that is committed to achieving the values and principles of the force.

- The opportunity to learn new skills.

Poor reasons to give:

- The pay and pension.

- The leave or holiday that you will get.

- Wearing a uniform, which ultimately means you don't have to pay for your own work clothes.

- Catching criminals and driving a police car.

What do you know about the role?

After studying this guide you will know a considerable amount about the role of a police officer. Before the final interview you must carry out plenty of research into the role and what the force will expect of you as a serving police officer.

Remember that the role is predominantly based around the core competencies, so be fully familiar with them before you attend the interview. It is also advisable that you study the 'Police Could You?' website, your recruitment literature, and also the website of the force you are applying to join.

Application form

During the final interview the panel may ask you questions that relate to your application form. In a previous section of this book we advised you to make sure you photocopy your application form prior to sending it off.

Before you attend the final interview familiarise yourself with the contents of your form and be prepared for any questions that you may be asked relating to it.

What you know about the force you are applying to join

During the final interview there is a strong possibility that you will be asked questions that relate to the force you are applying to join.

The following sample questions are the types that have been asked during final interviews in the past:

Q. What is it that has attracted you to this particular force?

Q. What can you tell me about the structure of this force?

Q. What can you tell me about the geographical area of this force?

Q. Can you tell me how this force is doing in relation to crime reduction?

Q. What crime reduction activities is this force currently involved in?

Q. What is neighbourhood policing and how does this force approach it?

Q. What is the 'policing pledge' and how is this force committed to it?

Q. What are the ambitions of this force?

Q. Who are our partners and stakeholders?

In order to prepare for questions that relate to the force you are applying to join, your first port of call is its website. From here you will be able to find out a considerable amount of information about its structure and activities, including the policing pledge and its success in driving down crime.

You may also wish to consider contacting your local police station and asking if it is possible to talk to a serving police officer about his or her role and the activities that the force is currently engaged in.

Situational interview questions

During the final interview the panel may ask you questions that relate to how you would respond or act in a given situation. This type of question is called a 'situational' type question.

Your response to each situational question must be 'specific' in nature. This means that you must provide an example where you have already been in this type of situation. During your response you should provide details of how you handled or dealt with the situation, preferably with a successful outcome.

Do not fall into the trap of providing a 'generic' response that details what you 'would do' if the situation arose, unless of course you have not been in this type of situation before.

When responding to situational questions structure your responses in a logical and concise manner. The way to achieve this is to use the 'STAR' method of interview question response construction:

Situation

Start off your response to the interview question by explaining what the 'situation' was and who was involved.

Task

Once you have detailed the situation, explain what the 'task' was, or what needed to be done.

Action

Now explain what 'action' you took, and what action others took. Also explain why you took this particular course of action.

Result

Explain what the outcome or result was following your actions and those of others. Try to demonstrate in your response that the result was positive because of the action you took.

Finally, explain to the panel what you would do differently if the same situation arose again. It is good to be reflective at the end of your responses. This demonstrates a level of

maturity and it will also show the panel that you are willing to learn from every experience.

Now that we have looked into how to prepare for the final interview, it is time to provide you with a number of sample questions and answers. Please note that the questions provided here are for practice purposes only and are not to be relied upon to be the exact questions that you will be asked during your final interview.

Sample final interview questions and sample responses

Sample question I

Tell us why you want to become a police officer.

I have worked in my current role now for a number of years. I have an excellent employer and enjoy working for them but unfortunately no longer find my job challenging. I understand that the role of a police officer is both demanding and rewarding and I believe I have the qualities to thrive in such an environment. I love working under pressure, working as part of a team that is diverse in nature and helping people in difficult situations. The public expectations of the police are very high and I believe I have the right qualities to help the police deliver the right service to the community.

I have studied the police core competencies and believe that I have the skills to match them and deliver what they require.

Top Tips

- Don't be negative about your current or previous employer.

- Be positive, enthusiastic and upbeat in your response.

- Make reference to the core competencies if possible.

Sample question 2

Why have you chosen this particular Police Force?

I have carried out extensive research into the Police Service and in particular this force. I have been impressed by the level of service it provides. The website provides the community with direct access to a different range of topics and the work that is being carried out through your community wardens is impressive. I have looked at the national and local crime statistics and read many different newspapers and articles.

I like this Police Force because of its reputation and the police officers that I have spoken to have told me that they get a great deal of job satisfaction from working here.

> **Top Tips**
> - Research the force thoroughly and make reference to particular success stories that they have achieved.
> - Be positive, enthusiastic and upbeat in your response.
> - Be positive about their force and don't be critical of it, even if you think it needs improving in certain areas.

Sample question 3

What does the role of a police officer involve?

Before I carried out my research and looked into the role of the police officer, I had the normal, stereotypical view of a police officer in that they catch criminals and reduce crime for a living.

While there is an element of that in the job, the police officer's role is far more diverse and varied. For example, they are there to serve the community and reduce the element of fear. They do this by communicating with their communities and being visible wherever possible.

They may need to pay particular attention to a person or groups of people who are the victims of crime or hatred. Therefore, the role of a police officer is both physically and psychologically to protect the community that they are serving.

It is also their role to work with other organisations such as the Fire Service, Social Services and other public sector bodies to try to reduce crime in a co-ordinated response as opposed to on their own.

Top Tips

- Understand the police core competencies and be able to recite them word for word.

- Understand the terms 'community policing' and 'policing pledge'.

Sample question 4

If one of the members of your team was gay and they told you this over a cup of tea at work, how do you think you would react?

I would have no problem at all. A person's sexual preference is their right and they should not be treated any differently for this. My attitude towards them and our working relationship would not be affected in any way. I have always treated everyone with respect and dignity at all times and will continue to do so throughout my career.

Top Tips

- Understand everything there is to know about equality and fairness. If you do not believe in it then this job is not for you.

- Visit the website www.gay.police.uk.

Sample question 5

If you were given an order that you thought was incorrect would you carry it out?

Yes I would. I would always respect my senior officers and their decisions.

However, if I thought something could be done in a better way then I do think that it is important to put it across, but in a structured and non-confrontational manner. During a debrief would probably be an appropriate time to offer up my views and opinions, if asked, but I would never refuse to carry out an order or even question it during an operational incident or otherwise.

Sample question 6

What do you understand by the term 'equality and fairness'?

It is an unfortunate fact that certain groups in society are still more likely to suffer from unfair treatment and discrimination. It is important for the Police Force and its staff to strive to eliminate all forms of unfair treatment and discrimination on the grounds that are specified in their policies or codes of practice.

'Equality and fairness' is the working culture in which fair treatment of all is the norm.

Top Tips

- Read the Police Force's policy on equality and fairness. You may be able to find this by visiting the website or asking for a copy of the policy to help you in your preparation.

- Consider reading the Race Relations Act, and understand the duties that are placed upon public sector organisations such as the police.

Sample question 7

How do you think the police could recruit more people from ethnic minority groups?

To begin with, it is important that police forces continue to build effective public relations. This can be achieved through certain avenues such as the force's website or even the local press. If the Police Force has a community liaison officer then this would be a good way to break down any barriers in the communities that we want to recruit from.

Another option is to ask people from these specific groups how they view this Police Force and what they think we could do to recruit more people from their community. Along with this it may be an option to focus media campaigns where there are higher populations of ethnic minority groups.

Comprehensive list of interview questions to prepare for

Q. Why do you want to become a police officer?

Q. What are your strengths?

Q. What are your weaknesses?

Q. What can you tell us about this particular Police Force?

Q. What do you understand by the term 'teamwork'?

Q. What makes an effective team?

Q. Why would you make a good police officer?

Q. What do you think the role of a police officer entails?

Q. If you saw a colleague being bullied or harassed, what would you do?

Q. What do you think are the qualities of an effective police officer?

Q. If one of your colleagues told you that they were gay, how would you react?

Q. What have you done so far to find out about the role of a police officer?

Q. Why do you want to join this particular Police Force?

Q. Give examples of when you have had to work in a team.

Q. What would you do if a member of your team was not pulling their weight or doing their job effectively?

Q. Have you ever had to defuse a confrontational situation? What did you do and what did you say?

Q. What are the main issues affecting the police at this current time?

Q. What do you understand about the term 'equality and fairness'?

Q. What do you understand by the term 'equal opportunities'?

Q. If you ever heard a racist or sexist remark, what would you do?

Q. Would you say that you are a motivated person?

Q. How do you keep yourself motivated?

Q. Have you ever had to work as part of a team to achieve a common goal?

Q. If you were in the canteen at work and two senior officers began to make homophobic comments, what would you do?

Q. Have you ever made a poor decision? If so, what was it?

Q.   If you were ever given an order that you thought was incorrect what would you do?

Q.   Have you ever had to work with somebody that you dislike?

Q.   What is wrong with your current job? Why do you want to leave it to become a police officer?

Q.   Have you ever carried out a project from beginning to end?

Q.   How do you think you would cope with the anti-social working hours?

Q.   Have you ever had to work shifts?

Q.   How do you think you would cope with working the police shift system?

Further Tips and Advice

- The police panel may ask you more generic questions relating to your past experiences or skills. These may be in relation to solving problems, working as an effective team member, dealing with difficult or aggressive people and defusing confrontational situations. Make sure you have examples for each of these.

- Speak to current serving police officers of the force that you are applying to join. Ask them what it is like to work for that particular force and what the current policing issues are. From their feedback take the positive points but don't use any detrimental or negative feedback during the interview.

- Think of a time when you have made a mistake and how you learnt from the experience.

- When you complete the application form make sure you keep a copy of it. Before you go to your interview ensure that you read the application form over and over again as you may find you are asked questions about your responses.

- Don't be afraid to ask the interviewer to repeat a question if you do not hear it the first time. Take your time when answering and be measured in your responses.

- If you don't know the answer to a question then be honest and just say 'I don't know'. This is far better than trying to answer a question that you have no knowledge about. Conversely, if your answer to a question is challenged there is nothing wrong with sticking to your point but make sure you acknowledge the interviewer's thoughts or views. Be polite and never get into a debate.

- You will be scored against the current police core competencies so make sure you structure your answers accordingly. The police core competencies are the first thing you should learn during your preparation.

CHAPTER 12

FREQUENTLY ASKED QUESTIONS RELATING TO THE FINAL INTERVIEW

Q. How long will my interview last?

A. Of course, this very much depends on how long your responses are.

Generally, the interview will last between 45 and 60 minutes.

Top Tips

- Make sure you drink plenty of water during the day before the interview. This will help your mind to stay focused and also keep you hydrated during your interview.

- Avoid alcohol the day before the interview and certainly do not have a drink on the day of the interview. While this may help to calm your nerves, the panel will be able to smell alcohol on your breath.

Q. Do you think I should ask questions at the end of my interview?

A. This can't do any harm providing that the questions aren't inappropriate or harmful to your chances of success. Questions such as 'Thank you for taking the time to interview me; can you tell me what the next stage is please?' are satisfactory questions.

However, questions such as 'I have read that the Police Force in this area has been criticised for its poor crime reduction figures lately; what are the police going to do about it?' are definitely not advised. Do not try to be clever!

Top Tips

- Be smart. Tidy hair, clean shoes and a suit all create a good image.

- Spend time sitting up straight in a chair at home and pretend that you are being interviewed.

- Carry out a mock interview prior to your actual interview day.

- When answering questions respond to the panel as opposed to the person who has asked you the question.

- Make eye contact with the members of the panel as opposed to looking at the floor. However, don't be aggressive in your eye contact.

Q. Is it all right to use 'body language' during my interview to express myself?

A. Yes, most definitely.

Using your hands or facial expression during any interview is a positive aspect as it demonstrates confidence. However, there is a fine line between subtle expression and overdoing it. If it becomes too obvious then it can be off-putting for the

panel. Try sitting in front of a mirror and practise saying the reasons why you want to become a police officer. This will give you an idea of what the panel will be looking at during your interview.

Top Tips

• Sit up straight in the chair at all times and do not slouch.

• Smile whenever possible and be confident.

• Rest the palms of your hands on your knees when you are not using them to express yourself and keep your feet flat on the ground.

Q. What are the scoring criteria for the final police officer interview?

A. Don't get tied down or concerned with specific pass marks or pass rates.

The police will score you using their own criteria. Where possible, structure your responses to the interview questions around the core competencies.

You may find some of the following phrases useful when constructing your answers:

• dignity and respect

• team working

• strong working relationships

• effective team member

• achieving common goals

• customer focus

• community policing

• policing pledge

- sensitive to cultural issues
- sensitive towards racial differences
- presenting the right image to the public
- effective communication
- identify problems and make effective decisions
- motivated, conscientious and committed
- calm, considerate and can work well under pressure

CHAPTER 13

THE POLICE OFFICER FITNESS TEST

The fitness test stage of the police selection process covers two specific areas.

These are:

- the endurance test or multi-stage fitness test

- the dynamic strength test.

On the following pages I have provided you with information relating to each of the two individual sections but it is important that you check with the force you are applying to join that the information is correct.

The police fitness test is not too difficult but obviously this will very much depend on your own abilities. With a degree of focused preparation you can pass the police fitness test with relative ease. Use the 'How to Get Police Officer Fit' bonus section during your preparation.

You may also wish to purchase the actual endurance test/bleep test audio CD from our online shop at www.how2become. co.uk. This CD is very similar to the test used by the police and you will find it a useful tool in your preparation.

The endurance test

The endurance test, also known as the 'multi-stage fitness test', 'bleep' or 'shuttle run' test, is often used by sports coaches and trainers to estimate an athlete's VO2 Max (maximum oxygen uptake). Apart from the police, the test is also used by the Armed Forces, Emergency Services and Prison Service as part of their selection process, but it is also a great way to improve and monitor your own fitness level.

Description

The 'bleep' test involves running continuously between two points that are 15 m apart (20 m in some cases). These 'shuttle' runs are done in time to pre-recorded 'bleep' sounds on an audio CD or cassette. The time between the recorded 'bleeps' decreases after each minute and, therefore, the test becomes progressively harder with each level completed. The full test consists of approximately 23 levels but the actual police endurance test only requires you to achieve four shuttles at level 5 to pass. Each level lasts approximately 60 seconds.

A level is basically a series of 15 m 'shuttle runs'. The starting speed is normally 8.5 km/h, which then increases by 0.5 km/h with each new level.

To purchase your copy of the bleep test, please visit www. how2become.co.uk.

The dynamic strength test

This test mimics a seated bench press action and a seated rowing action. You will be asked to perform five repetitions on

both the push and pull aspects. The machine works out the average of your five repetitions and gives you a score. You must push 34 kg and pull 35 kg to pass.

Two of the most effective ways to prepare for this type of test include rowing (using a rowing machine) and press-ups. The reason why I recommend rowing during your preparation is that apart from increasing your physical strength it will also help prepare you for the endurance test.

Within the 'How to Get Police Officer Fit' guide I have provided some useful tips and exercises.

IMPORTANT: Make sure you consult a medical practitioner prior to engaging in any strenuous physical exercise programme.

FREE BONUS GUIDE – HOW TO GET POLICE OFFICER FIT

Introduction

Welcome to your FREE 'How to Get Police Officer Fit' information guide. Within this guide I have provided a number of useful exercises that will allow you to prepare for, and pass, the police officer fitness tests.

The police officer fitness test is not difficult to pass, providing you put in the time and effort to reach a good all-round level of fitness. Police officers need to have a good all-round aerobic fitness and also a good level of strength and stamina. The exercises contained within this guide will help you to achieve exactly that. Do not spend hours in the gym lifting heavy weights as the job does not require that level of strength, but rather aim for a varied and diverse fitness programme that covers exercises such as swimming, rowing, jogging, brisk walking and light weight work.

In addition to getting fit, keep an eye on your diet and try to eat healthy foods while drinking plenty of water. It will all go a long way to helping you improve your general well-being and concentration levels while you prepare for the selection process.

Planning your workouts and preparing for the police officer fitness tests

Most people who embark on a fitness regime in January have given it up by February. The reason why most people give up their fitness regime so soon is mainly owing to a lack of proper preparation. You will recall that throughout this book the word 'preparation' has been integral, and the same word applies when preparing for the fitness tests. Preparation is key to your success and it is essential that you plan your workouts effectively.

To begin with, think about the role of a police officer and what it entails. You will have to run pretty fast on some occasions and you will also need a level of strength for certain operational tasks. In the build-up to the physical tests I advise that you concentrate on specific exercises that will allow you to pass the tests with ease.

Read on for some great ways to pass the police officer fitness tests and stay fit all year round.

Get an assessment before you start training

The first step is to get a fitness test at the gym, weigh yourself and run your fastest mile. Once you have done all three of these you should write down your results and keep them hidden away somewhere safe. After a month of following your new fitness regime, do all three tests again and check your results against the previous month's. This is a great way to monitor your performance and progress and it will also keep you motivated and focused on your goals.

Keep a check on what you eat and drink

Make sure you write down everything you eat and drink for a whole week. You must include tea, water, milk, biscuits, and anything and everything that you digest. You will soon begin to realise how much you are eating and you will notice areas in which you can make some changes. For example, if you are taking sugar with your tea then why not try reducing it or giving it up all together. If you do then you will soon notice the difference.

It is important that you start to look for opportunities to improve your fitness and well-being right from the offset. These areas are what I call 'easy wins'.

Exercises that will help you to pass the fitness tests

It is my strong belief that you do not have to attend a gym in order to prepare for the police officer fitness tests. If I was applying to become a police officer today then I would embark on a fitness programme that included brisk walking, running, rowing, presses, sit-ups, squats and lunges. In order to improve my upper body strength I would also go swimming.

Walking is one of the best exercises you can do as part of your preparation for the police officer fitness tests. While it shouldn't be the only form of exercise you carry out, it will go a long way to improving your focus and general well-being. Now, when I say 'walking' I don't mean a gentle stroll, I mean 'brisk' walking. Try walking at a fast pace for 30 minutes every day for a seven-day period. Then see how you feel at the end of the seven-day period. I guarantee you'll begin to feel a lot healthier and fitter. Brisk walking is also a fantastic way to lose weight if you think you need to. In addition to helping you to lose weight, it will also keep your concentration and motivational levels up.

There are some more great exercises contained within this guide and most of them can be carried out without the need to attend a gym.

One step at a time

Only you will know how fit you are. I advise that, first of all, you write down the areas that you believe or feel you need to improve on. For example, if you feel that you need to work on your upper body strength then pick out exercises from this guide that will work on that area for you. I also advise that you obtain a copy of the multi-stage fitness test and practise it. Make sure you can easily pass the required standard.

The key to making improvements is to do it gradually, and at one step at a time. Set yourself small goals. If you think you need to lose 2 stone (13 kg) in weight then focus on losing a few pounds at a time. For example, during the first month aim to lose 6 pounds (3 kg) only. Once you have achieved this then again aim to lose another 6 pounds over the next month, and so on and so forth. The more realistic your goal, the more likely you are to achieve it. One of the biggest problems that people encounter when starting a fitness regime is they become bored quickly. This then leads to a lack of motivation and desire, and soon the fitness programme stops.

Change your exercise routine often. Instead of walking try jogging. Instead of jogging try cycling with the odd day of swimming. Keep your workouts varied and interesting to ensure that you stay focused and motivated.

Stretching

How many people stretch before carrying out any form of exercise? Very few people is the correct answer. Not only is it irresponsible but it is also placing yourself at high risk from injury. Before we commence with the exercises we will take a look at a few warm-up stretches. Make sure you stretch fully before carrying out any exercises. You want your police

officer career to be a long one and that means looking after yourself, including stretching! It is also very important to check with your GP that you are medically fit to carry out any form of physical exercise.

The warm-up calf stretch

To perform this stretch effectively you should first start by facing a wall while standing upright. Your right foot should be close to the wall and your right knee bent. Now place your hands flat against the wall and at a height that is level with your shoulders. Stretch your left leg far out behind you without lifting your toes and heel off the floor, and lean towards the wall.

Once you have performed this stretch for 25 seconds, switch legs and carry out the same procedure for the left leg. As with all exercises contained within this guide, stop if you feel any pain or discomfort.

Stretching the shoulder muscles

To begin with, stand with your feet slightly apart and with your knees only slightly bent. Now hold your arms right out in front of you and with your palms facing away from you with your fingers pointing skywards. Now place your right palm on the back of your left hand and use it to push the left hand further away from you. If you are performing this exercise correctly then you will feel the muscles in your shoulder stretching. Hold for 10 seconds before switching sides.

Stretching the quad muscles (front of the thigh)

Before you carry out any form of brisk walking or running then it is imperative that you stretch your leg muscles. During the police officer fitness tests, and especially prior to the multi-stage fitness test, the instructors should take you through a series of warm-up exercises which will include stretching

the quad muscles. To begin with, stand with your right hand pressed against the back of a wall or firm surface. Bend your left knee and bring your left heel up to your bottom while grasping your foot with your left hand. Your back should be straight and your shoulders, hips and knees should all be in line at all times during the exercise. Hold for 25 seconds before switching legs.

Stretching the hamstring muscles (back of the thigh)

To perform this exercise correctly, stand up straight and place your right foot onto a table or other firm surface so that your leg is almost parallel to the floor. Keep your left leg straight and your foot at a right angle to your leg. Start to slowly move your hands down your right leg towards your ankle until you feel tension on the underside of your thigh. When you feel this tension you know that you are starting to stretch the hamstring muscles. Hold for 25 seconds before switching legs.

We have covered only a small number of stretching exercises here; however, it is crucial that you stretch out fully in all areas before carrying out any of the following exercises. Remember to obtain professional advice before carrying out any type of exercise.

Running

As I have already mentioned, one of the great ways to prepare for the police officer fitness tests is to embark on a structured running programme. You do not need to run at a fast pace, or even run for long distances, in order to gain massively from this type of exercise.

Before I joined the Fire Service I spent a few years in the Royal Navy. I applied to join the Navy when I was 16 and I made it through the selection process with ease until I reached the medical. During the medical the doctor told me that I was overweight and that I had to lose a stone before they would accept me. To be honest, I was heart-broken. I couldn't believe

it, especially after all that hard work I had put in preparing for the tests and the interview! Anyway, as soon as I arrived back home from the medical I started out on a structured running programme that would see me lose the stone in weight within only four weeks! The following running programme is very similar to one I used all those years ago and it will serve you well when preparing for the police officer fitness tests.

Before I provide you with the running programme, however, read the following important running tips.

Tips for Running

- As with any exercise you should consult a doctor before taking part to make sure that you are medically fit.

- It is certainly worth investing in a pair of comfortable running shoes that serve the purpose for your intended training programme. Your local sports shop will be able to advise you on the types that are best for you. You don't have to spend a fortune to buy a good pair of running shoes.

- It is a good idea to invest in a 'high visibility' jacket or coat so that you can be seen by fast-moving traffic if you intend to run on or near the road.

- Make sure you carry out at least five whole minutes of stretching exercises not only before but also after your running programme. This can help to prevent injury.

- While you shouldn't run on a full stomach, it is also not good to run on an empty one either. A great food to eat approximately 30 minutes before a run is a banana. This is excellent for giving you energy.

- Drink plenty of water throughout the day. Try to drink at least 1.5 litres each day in total. This will keep you hydrated and help to prevent muscle cramp.

- Don't overdo it. If you feel any pain or discomfort then stop and seek medical advice.

Running programme week 1

DAY 1

- Run a total of 3 miles only at a steady pace.

If you cannot manage 3 miles then try the following:

- Walk at a brisk pace for half a mile or approximately 10 minutes.

½ MILE WALK / 10 MIN

Then

- Run for 1 mile or 8 minutes.

Then

- Walk for another half a mile or approximately 10 minutes.

Then

- Run for 1.5 miles or 12 minutes.

Walking at a brisk pace is probably the most effective way to lose weight if you need to. It is possible to burn the same amount of calories if you walk the same distance as if you were running.

When walking at a 'brisk' pace it is recommended that you walk as fast as is comfortably possible without breaking into a run or slow jog.

DAY 2

- Walk for 2 miles or approximately 20 minutes at a brisk pace.

Then

- Run for 2 miles or 14 minutes.

DAY 3

- Repeat Day 1.

DAY 4

- Walk at a brisk pace for 0.5 miles or approximately 7 minutes.

Then

- Run for 3 miles or 20 minutes.

DAY 5

- Repeat Day 1.

DAY 6 AND DAY 7

- Rest days. No exercise.

Running programme week 2

DAY 1

- Run for 4 miles or 25 minutes.

DAY 2

- Run a total of 3 miles at a steady pace.

If you cannot manage 3 miles then try the following:

- Walk at a brisk pace for half a mile or approximately 10 minutes.

Then

- Run for 1 mile or 8 minutes.

Then

- Walk for another half a mile or approximately 10 minutes.

Then

- Run for 1.5 miles or 12 minutes.

DAY 3

- Rest day. No exercise.

DAY 4

- Run for 5 miles or 35–40 minutes.

DAY 5

- Run for 3 miles or 20 minutes.

Then

- Walk at a brisk pace for 2 miles or approximately 20 minutes.

DAY 6

- Run for 5 miles or 35–45 minutes.

DAY 7

- Rest day. No exercise.

Once you have completed the second week running programme, use the third week to perform different types of exercises, such as cycling and swimming. During week 4 you can then commence the two-week running programme again. You'll be amazed at how much easier it is the second time around!

When preparing for the police officer selection process, use your exercise time as a break from your studies. For example, if you have been working on the application form for a couple of hours why not take a break and go running? When you return from your run you can then concentrate on your studies feeling refreshed.

Now that I've provided you with a structured running programme to follow, there really are no excuses. So, get out there and start running! I'll now provide you with a number of key targeted exercises that will allow you to prepare effectively for the police officer fitness tests.

Exercises that will improve your ability to pass the police officer fitness tests

Press-ups

While running is a great way to improve your overall fitness, you will also need to carry out exercises that improve your upper body strength. These exercises will help you to pass the strength tests which form part of the assessment. The great thing about press-ups is that you don't have to attend a gym to perform them. However, you must ensure that you can do them correctly as injury can occur. You only need to spend five minutes every day on press-ups, possibly after you go running or even before if you prefer. If you are not used to doing press-ups then start slowly and aim to carry out at least ten.

Even if you struggle to do just ten, you will soon find that after a few days' practice at these you will be up to 20 or more.

Step 1 – To begin with, lie on a mat or even surface. Your hands should be shoulder width apart and your arms fully extended.

Step 2 – Gradually lower your body until the elbows reach 90°. Do not rush the movement as you may cause injury.

Step 3 – Once your elbows reach 90° slowly return to the starting position with your arms fully extended.

The press-up action should be a continuous movement with no rest. However, it is important that the exercise is as smooth as possible and there should be no jolting or sudden movements. Try to complete as many press-ups as possible and always keep a record of how many you do. This will keep your focus and also maintain your motivation levels.

Did you know that the world record for non-stop press-ups is currently 10,507 set in 1980?

WARNING – Ensure you take advice from a competent fitness trainer in relation to the correct execution of press-up exercises and other exercises contained within this guide.

Sit-ups

Sit-ups are great for building the core stomach muscles. At the commencement of the exercise lie flat on your back with your knees bent at a 45° angle and with your feet together. Your hands can either be crossed on your chest, by your sides, or cupped behind your ears as indicated in the diagram opposite.

Without moving your lower body, curl your upper torso upwards and in towards your knees, until your shoulder blades are as high off the ground as possible. As you reach the highest point, tighten your abdominal muscles for a second. This will allow you to get the most out of the exercise. Now slowly start to lower yourself back to the starting position. You should be aiming to work up to at least 50 effective sit-ups every day. You will be amazed at how quickly this can be achieved and you will begin to notice your stomach muscles developing.

While sit-ups do not form part of police officer fitness tests, they are still a great way of improving your all-round fitness and therefore should not be neglected.

Pull-ups

Pull-ups are another great way for building the core upper body muscle groups. The unfortunate thing about this type of exercise is you will probably need to attend a gym in order to carry them out. Having said that, there are a number of different types of 'pull-up bars' available to buy on the market that can be fitted easily and safely to a doorway at home. If you choose to purchase one of these items make sure that it conforms to the relevant safety standards first.

Lateral pull-ups are very effective at increasing upper body strength. If you have access to a gymnasium then these can be practised on a 'lateral pull-down' machine. It is advised that you consult a gym member of staff about how to do these exercises.

Pull-ups should be performed by grasping firmly a sturdy and solid bar. Before you grasp the bar make sure it is safe. Your hands should be roughly shoulder-width apart. Straighten your arms so that your body hangs loose. You will feel your lateral muscles and biceps stretching as you hang in the air. This is the starting position for the lateral pull-up exercise.

Next, pull yourself upwards to the point where your chest is almost touching the bar and your chin is actually over the bar. While pulling upwards, focus on keeping your body straight without any arching or swinging as this can result in injury. Once

your chin is over the bar, you can lower yourself back down to the initial starting position. Repeat the exercise ten times.

Squats (these work the legs and bottom)

Squats are a great exercise for working the leg muscles. They are the perfect exercise in your preparation for the police officer fitness tests.

At the commencement of the exercise, stand up straight with your arms at your sides. Concentrate on keeping your feet shoulder-width apart and your head up. Do not look downwards at any point during the exercise. You will see from the diagram that the person has their lower back slightly arched. They are also holding light weights which can add to the intensity of the exercise.

Now start to bend your knees very slowly while pushing your rear out as though you are about to sit down on a chair. Keep

lowering yourself down until your thighs reach past the 90° point. Make sure your weight is on your heels so that your knees do not extend over your toes. At this point you may wish to tighten your thighs and buttocks to intensify the exercise.

As you come back up to a standing position, push down through your heels which will allow you to maintain your balance. Repeat the exercise 15 to 20 times.

Lunges (these work the thighs and bottom)

You will have noticed throughout this section of the guide that I have been providing you with simple, yet highly effective exercises that can be carried out at home. The lunge exercise is another great addition to the range of exercises that require no attendance at the gym.

To begin with, stand with your back straight and your feet together (you may hold light hand weights if you wish to add some intensity to the exercise).

Next, take a big step forwards as illustrated in the diagram opposite making sure you inhale as you go and landing with the heel first. Bend the front knee no more than 90° so as to avoid injury. Keep your back straight and lower the back knee as close to the floor as possible. Your front knee should be lined up over your ankle and your back thigh should be in line with your back.

To complete the exercise, exhale and push down against your front heel, squeezing your buttocks tight as you rise back to a starting position.

Try to repeat the exercise 15 to 20 times before switching sides.

Lateral raises (these work the shoulder muscles)

While police officers are not usually required to lift heavy items of equipment during their day-to-day work, they still need to have a good level of upper body strength. Lateral raises will allow you to improve your upper body strength in a safe and effective manner.

Take a dumbbell in each hand and hold them by the sides of your body with the palms facing inward.

Stand or sit with your feet shoulder-width apart, knees slightly bent. Do not lean backwards as you could cause injury to your back. Raise your arms up and out to the sides (as shown in the diagram on the following page) until they are parallel to the ground, then lower them back down carefully. Repeat the exercise 15 to 20 times.

Alternative exercises

Swimming

Apart from press-ups, lateral raises and the other exercises I have provided, another fantastic way to improve your upper body and overall fitness is to go swimming. If you have access to a swimming pool, and you can swim, then this is a brilliant way to improve your fitness.

If you are not a great swimmer you can start off with short distances and gradually build up your swimming strength and stamina. Breaststroke is sufficient for building good upper body strength providing you put the effort into swimming an effective number of lengths. You may wish to alternate your running programme with the odd day of swimming. If you can swim 10 lengths of a 25 m pool initially then this is a good base to start from. You will soon find that you can increase this number easily providing that you carry on swimming every week. Try running to your local swimming pool if it is not too far away, swimming 20 lengths of breaststroke, and then running back home.

This is a great way to combine your fitness activity and prevent yourself from becoming bored with your training programme.

Rowing

If there is one exercise that will allow you to work every single muscle group in the body then it is rowing. This is the perfect exercise for preparing to pass the police officer fitness tests. It will increase your aerobic fitness and it will also improve your lower and upper body strength.

As with any exercise of this nature there is a risk of injury. It is crucial that you use the correct technique when rowing on a purpose-built machine. By applying the correct technique you will be far more efficient and you will also see faster results.

While exercising on the rowing machine, make sure you keep your back straight and concentrate on using your legs and buttocks. Never extend so far that you lock out your knees. Try to keep the action smooth throughout the entire exercise. To obtain a suitable indoor rowing training programme that is relevant to your current fitness levels, please visit www. concept2.co.uk.

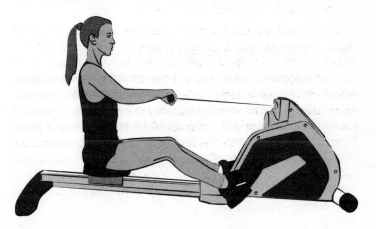

The multi-stage fitness test or bleep test

This part of the police officer selection process requires you to demonstrate a specific level of fitness.

In simple terms the bleep test requires you to run backwards and forwards (shuttles) between two fixed points a set distance apart. The test is progressive in that as the levels increase so does the difficulty. A tape will be played that contains a series of 'bleeps' set out at different intervals.

The time between the 'bleeps' at level 1 will be far greater than the 'bleeps' at level 10. Each time the 'bleeps' increase, the tape will let you know that you are progressing to the next level. During the test you will be required to keep up with 'bleeps' and not fall behind them or run ahead of them. Level 1 starts off at around walking pace and gradually increases as each stage progresses.

The best way to practise for this stage of the test is to practise the actual test itself. However, the next best alternative is to go running at 3 miles, at least three times a week. Each time you go out running you should try to push yourself a little bit harder and further.

By running three times a week you will give your body the rest it needs in between each run, so it is probably best to run on alternate days.

Tips for staying with your workout

The hardest part of your training programme will be sticking with it. In this final part of your fitness guide I will provide some useful golden rules that will enable you to maintain your motivational levels in the build-up to the police officer fitness tests. In order to stay with your workout for longer, try following these simple rules:

Golden rule number one – Work out often

Aim to train three to five times each and every week.

Each training session should last between 20 minutes to a maximum of an hour. The quality of training is important so don't go for heavy weights but instead go for a lighter weight with a better technique. On days when you are feeling energetic, take advantage of this opportunity and do more!

Within this guide I have deliberately provided you with a number of 'simple to perform' exercises that are targeted at the core muscle groups required to perform the role of a police officer. In between your study sessions try carrying out these exercises at home or get yourself out on road running or cycling. Use your study 'down time' effectively and wisely.

Golden rule number two – Mix up your exercises

Your exercise programme should include some elements of cardiovascular (aerobics, running, brisk walking and cycling), resistance training (weights or own body exercises such as press-ups and sit-ups) and, finally, flexibility (stretching). Make sure that you always warm up and warm down.

If you are a member of a gym then consider taking up a class such as Pilates. This form of exercise class will teach you how to build core training into your exercise principles, and show you how to hit your abdominals in ways that are not possible with conventional sit-ups. If you are a member of a gym then a fantastic 'all round' exercise that I strongly recommend is rowing. Rowing will hit every major muscle group in your body and it is also perfect for improving your stamina levels and cardiovascular fitness.

Golden rule number three – Eat a healthy and balanced diet

It is vitally important that you eat the right fuel to give you the energy to train to your full potential. Don't fill your body with

rubbish and then expect to train well. Think about what you are eating and drinking, including the quantities, and keep a record of what you are digesting. You will become stronger and fitter more quickly if you eat little amounts of nutritious foods at short intervals.

Golden rule number four – Get help

Try working with a personal trainer. They will ensure that you work hard and will help you to achieve your goals. If you cannot afford a personal trainer then try training with someone else. The mere fact that they are there at your side will add an element of competition to your training sessions!

A consultation with a professional nutritionist will also help you improve your eating habits and establish your individual food needs.

Golden rule number five – Fitness is for life

One of my old managers in the Fire Service had a saying – 'Fitness Wins!' Two simple words, that meant an awful lot. Improving your fitness and eating healthily are not short-term projects. They are things that should come naturally to you.

Make fitness a permanent part of your life by following these tips, and you'll lead a better and more fulfilling life!

Good luck and work hard to improve your weak areas.

A FEW FINAL WORDS

You have now reached the end of the guide and no doubt you will be ready to start preparing for the police officer selection process. Just before you go off and start on your preparation, consider the following.

The majority of candidates who pass the police officer selection process have a number of common attributes. These are as follows:

They believe in themselves

Regardless of what anyone tells you, you *can* become a police officer. Just like any job of this nature, you have to be prepared to work hard in order to be successful. Make sure you have the self-belief to pass the selection process and fill your mind with positive thoughts.

They prepare fully

Those people who achieve in life prepare fully for every eventuality and that is what you must do when you apply

to become a police officer. Work very hard and especially concentrate on your weak areas.

They persevere

Perseverance is a fantastic word. Everybody comes across obstacles or setbacks in their life, but it is what you do about those setbacks that is important. If you fail at something, then ask yourself 'why' you have failed. This will allow you to improve for next time and if you keep improving and trying, success will eventually follow. Apply this same method of thinking when you apply to become a police officer.

They are self-motivated

How much do you want this job? Do you want it, or do you *really* want it?

When you apply to join the police you should want it more than anything in the world. Your levels of self-motivation will shine through on your application and during your interview. For the weeks and months leading up to the police officer selection process, be motivated as best you can and always keep your fitness levels up as this will serve to increase your levels of motivation.

Work hard, stay focused and be what you want . . .

Richard McMunn

INDEX

Visit www.how2become.co.uk to find more related products that will help you to pass this selection process. From the website we can provide you with DVDs and guides that will help you to pass the interview, and other stages of the selection process. We also run one-day intensive training courses that are designed to help you successfully pass the application process for any career.

Visit www.how2become.co.uk for more details.

INTERVIEW

4 INTERACTIVE EXERCISES

2 WRITTEN EXERCISES

NUMERICAL TEST

VERBAL TEST